Israel
for Perplexed
Beginners

A Crash Course
in Understanding Israelis

Angelo Colorni

gefen
publishing house בית הוצאה לאור
JERUSALEM ♦ NEW YORK   Est. 1981

Typesetting: Optume Technologies

ISBN: 978-965-229-960-4

1 3 5 7 9 8 6 4 2

Gefen Publishing House Ltd.
6 Hatzvi Street
Jerusalem 9438614, Israel
972-2-538-0247
orders@gefenpublishing.com

Gefen Books
140 Fieldcrest Ave.
Edison NJ, 08837
516-593-1234
orders@gefenpublishing.com

Library of Congress Cataloging-in-Publication Data

Names: Colorni, Angelo, author.
Title: Israel for perplexed beginners : a crash course in understanding Israelis /
    Angelo Colorni.
Description: Jerusalem, Israel : Gefen Publishing House Ltd. ; Edison NJ :
    Gefen Books, [2018]
Identifiers: LCCN 2018021715 | ISBN 9789652299604
Subjects: LCSH: Israeli wit and humor. | Israel—Social life and customs—Humor. |
    Israelis—Social life and customs—Humor.
Classification: LCC PN6222.I8 C65 2018 | DDC 892.447—dc23
LC record available at https://lccn.loc.gov/2018021715

www.gefenpublishing.com

Printed in Israel

Contents

Foreword

After *Israel for Beginners* (Gefen, 2011) and *Israel for Advanced Beginners* (Steimatzky, 2015), this last burst of benevolent fun poked at my fellow Israelis, *Israel for Perplexed Beginners*, completes the trilogy. Some friends laughed at my ambition to become a humorist. This is the third humorous book I have written; nobody's laughing now.

I chose the title *Israel for Perplexed Beginners* for this last book, even though the term *perplexed* is often a euphemistic understatement for the state of mind of those of you who decided to leave a presumably comfortable existence in familiar surroundings and give your lives a new start in Israel. Confused, bewildered, and lost in a maze of novel idiosyncrasies beyond your comprehension, you are going through an unavoidable initial period that you will later refer to as "culture shock." This initial period of adjustment may last well into your third and – if you reach it – fourth age. Actually, you may find yourself still working on it after that. On the bright side, it makes you realize why the difficult task of living your life has never been attempted by anyone else before.

Ubi Cor, Ibi Patria: Making *Aliyah*

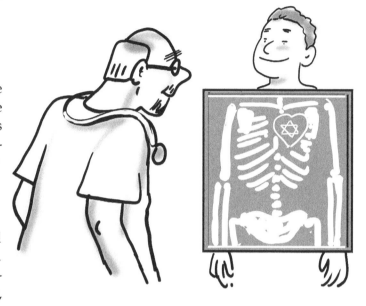

You relocated from the country in which you were born, grew up, had friends and relatives, had a mentality and lifestyle similar to that of your compatriots, spoke their language, had a fairly equal chance in the labor market, and decided to come to Israel. So you made *aliyah* (literally "ascent" in Hebrew, symbolically meaning to immigrate to Israel), and you're now an *oleh chadash* or an *olah chadashah* (new immigrant). *Mazal tov* (congratulations)! You may be an odd bird, but you are not a rara avis. Some 40 percent of Israelis are immigrants. More globally speaking, in fact, every human has been a migrant or the descendant of migrants since Adam and Eve were unceremoniously kicked out of the Garden of Eden.

The window "Are you sure you want to do this?" popped up many times in your mind just as it does on your computer. Both the *OK* and *Cancel* options were just a click away, and with understandable apprehension, you pressed *OK*. You may not realize it, but you are making your dreams bigger than your fears, and you are beginning to live your life on your own terms. Be patient and gentle with yourself, and strive to keep your own individuality, to remain uniquely yourself. (Everyone else is taken anyway!)

Zionism: We're All Here Possibly because We're Not All Here

Relative to its population, Israel is the largest immigrant-absorbing nation on earth. Some immigrants come in search of religious fulfillment, others look for personal development, and others yet come looking for job opportunities. Most, however, are driven by the desire to maintain their Jewish identity and "feel at home" in a holistic Jewish society. Confronted with the huge security threats Israel is facing, prospective immigrants might be expected to be discouraged and veteran Israelis to flee abroad. Instead, Jews continue to make *aliyah*, many from Europe, where their safety and sense of security have been gradually eroding, while a contagious optimism prevails among the Israelis about their country's future.

Unquestionably, once you join the Israeli natives and give up on reality, all your perplexities dissipate, many new possibilities open up to you, and the meaning of life stands explained.

The Israeli Expats: Making *Yeridah*

You relocated from the country in which you were born, grew up, had friends and relatives, had a mentality and lifestyle similar to that of your compatriots, spoke their language, had a fairly equal chance in the labor market, and decided to leave Israel. So you made *yeridah* (literally "descent" in Hebrew, generally referring unsympathetically to the Israeli natives who emigrate from Israel) and you're now a displaced Israeli expat living somewhere in a foreign land across the globe.

The number of people who have emigrated from the State of Israel since its establishment has always been difficult to estimate. Today, Israel has one of the lowest emigration rates among developed countries. And yet, some pastures still seem greener abroad, and certain opportunities seem more easily realizable overseas. Driven by the ambition to improve living standards, whether in the form of better job prospects or of more rapid academic or professional advancement, disgruntled emigrants are ready to cross the ocean and work very hard to succeed. Indeed, they often go through – unfortunately in the opposite direction – the same harsh wilderness their ancestors crossed before reaching the Promised Land. Many eventually find the key to success. Few manage to find the lock.

The *yordim* (emigrants from Israel) proudly wave the Israeli flag, but they actually waive what it stands for. They come back to Israel sporadically to visit family and friends, cast their votes in legislative elections, and fight wars. They then return to their adoptive countries because they cannot do without the homesickness they feel for Israel from there.

3

Your Native Country in Your Heart

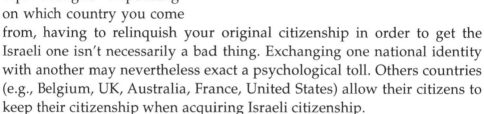

...and Israel in your soul. Countries vary in their attitudes toward dual citizenship. Some (e.g., Norway, Austria, China, Japan) reject the concept outright. Depending on which country you come from, having to relinquish your original citizenship in order to get the Israeli one isn't necessarily a bad thing. Exchanging one national identity with another may nevertheless exact a psychological toll. Others countries (e.g., Belgium, UK, Australia, France, United States) allow their citizens to keep their citizenship when acquiring Israeli citizenship.

If you became a dual citizen, you now carry two passports, likely of different colors. The Israeli one is blue and opens from (what you are used to considering) the wrong side. This double citizenship allows you to claim the benefits of Israeli citizenship without giving up the privileges and identity of your country of origin. No less important, you won't feel disloyal to the latter. As a first-generation immigrant, you will normally maintain a powerful emotional bond and strong ties to your country of birth and – finances permitting – you will travel quite frequently back and forth. One country is your homeland, and Israel your new home. The two passports make you feel that you belong and are welcome in both countries. There is no divided loyalty in this, but rather an expression of allegiance. If you are coming from another Western country in particular, you will probably be embracing the ideals and democratic ethos of both nations. On the plane that takes you to your native country for a visit, you will be thinking, "Wow, I'm going back home." On the plane that takes you back to Israel, you will be thinking, "Wow, I'm coming back home."

Being subject to the laws and regulations of both countries also means more personal accountability. The new life path you are now walking is your path and yours alone. Others may walk it with you, but no one can walk it for you. As a dual national, you are not considered a foreigner in Israel. If you are a young man of draft age, that includes complying with military obligations. So welcome home: you can pay Israeli taxes, vote in Israeli elections, wear an IDF uniform,[1] and fight in Israeli wars.

---

1. Israel Defense Forces (*Tzahal* in Hebrew, an acronym for *Tzva Ha-haganah Le-yisrael*).

Tracing Your Jewish Roots

Deep Roots Are Not Reached by either Frost or Scorching Sun

There is strength in our Jewish identity and strength in the depth of our Jewish roots in the Land of Israel. Like the branches of an old tree, we all grow in different directions. Yet the tree remains one, deeply rooted in our history, culture, language, and traditions. Each new generation is like the blossoming of new buds in spring that draw vital sap from those ancient roots, sprouting and becoming new branches, foliage, flowers, and fruits. From the green leaves of that old tree comes the oxygen we breathe.

The Law of Return, passed by the Knesset (Israeli Parliament) in 1950, is legislation that gives Jews from all over the world the right to live in Israel and be eligible for Israeli citizenship. In 1970, the law was extended to people of recent Jewish ancestry, inevitably rekindling the never-ending debate on "Who is a Jew." Israeli citizenship is granted if there is proven documentation that any grandparent was Jewish, since such a degree of connection was sufficient to be persecuted as Jews by the Nazis.[2] Thus, in an odd mix of vengeance and reverse logic, the definition of Jewishness is based on Nazi ideology rather than on strict *halakhic* (Jewish religious) criteria.

---

2. The Nuremberg Laws of 1935.

Abraham: The Jewish Family Tree Begins

For those who need documents to prove their Jewish pedigree, there are several genealogical research centers in Jerusalem.[3] You may start the search for your Jewish roots from there. Do not become frustrated if those of your forebears who could prove your Jewish ancestry seem to have all entered a witness protection program. At the same time, be prepared to find out that your family tree might have greatly gained from some healthy pruning now and then.

A more rapid alternative in your search for lost relatives would be to just win the top prize at the *Mifal Ha-pais* (Israel State Lottery), in which case your lost relatives will find you. Another more tortuous but surer approach would be to become a Knesset member; that way, your political opponents would conduct the genealogical research for you, eagerly singling out all the badly behaved ancestors in your family tree up to the time when your ancestors were actually hanging from your family tree.

---

3. E.g., Jewish Agency's Search Bureau for Missing Relatives, Yad Vashem, Central Archives for the History of the Jewish People. You may also want to start with MyHeritage, an online genealogy website.

Social Interactions with Israelis

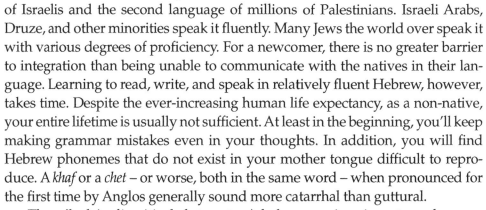

A Language with No Vowels

Israelis feel united and exclusive by speaking Hebrew. In the seventy years since the establishment of the State of Israel, Hebrew has become the mother tongue of millions of Israelis and the second language of millions of Palestinians. Israeli Arabs, Druze, and other minorities speak it fluently. Many Jews the world over speak it with various degrees of proficiency. For a newcomer, there is no greater barrier to integration than being unable to communicate with the natives in their language. Learning to read, write, and speak in relatively fluent Hebrew, however, takes time. Despite the ever-increasing human life expectancy, as a non-native, your entire lifetime is usually not sufficient. At least in the beginning, you'll keep making grammar mistakes even in your thoughts. In addition, you will find Hebrew phonemes that do not exist in your mother tongue difficult to reproduce. A *khaf* or a *chet* – or worse, both in the same word – when pronounced for the first time by Anglos generally sound more catarrhal than guttural.

The *nikud* (a diacritical dot system) helps new immigrants and young readers navigate through vowelless Hebrew. In manuals for learners, the marks corresponding to the vowels are placed above, below, or within a letter. In real life, the dots eventually come off, like bicycle training wheels, and you are left on your own to read and write in a language that does not consider vowels worthy of printing.

Cutting Short

Anglos cut corners by spelling *light* "lite" and *night* "nite." It is unclear what they do with all the time they save, but they are proud of sparing 20 percent of the letters. Savings can actually reach 66 percent when instead of *and* they use &, which, in any font, looks like a dog dragging his butt across the floor.

In Hebrew, writing words with as few letters as possible is taken to the extreme. For example, the word *lehitraot* (goodbye, see you soon) is often abbreviated as *lehit*; the word *likhvod* (to, for, in honor of), by itself not a particularly long word, is written as *likh*. Israel's capital, *Yerushalayim* in Hebrew, is often shortened as "Y—m."

You will quite often encounter words with a single quotation mark placed before the last letter. That indicates an acronym. Once you learn that words with quotation marks are not actual words but another time-saving element of Hebrew jargon,[4] you will use them frequently, believing that speaking like *sabras*[5] do speeds up your absorption.

Eventually, by continuously shortening words, the Israelis will be able to converse only in emojis, just as they do in instant messaging from their computers and smartphones. In other words, the evolution of communication will take them back to primordial times when our Stone Age ancestors overcame the communication barrier by exchanging signs, symbols, and grunts.[6]

English, So to Speak, Spoken Here

Native Israelis take pride in their ability to speak English, a language they absent-mindedly learn in school and often put to use during their almost de rigueur post-army trip in remote, exotic, non-Anglo-Saxon countries. Upon returning to Israel, they then use every available opportunity to practice their recently acquired language skills on their easiest target: new immigrants. Bad English has therefore become the unofficial second language of the State of Israel, both in its oral and written forms. This comes as a great consolation to self-conscious newcomers, who are often too concerned about inadvertently misusing words or grammatically abusing the true language of the Holy Bible. For example, while English uses the neuter gender to classify linguistically inanimate things, in Hebrew, everything is endowed with either a male or female soul. It is thus only natural for the natives to refer to things

---

4. Interestingly, some acronyms have been emancipated and were promoted to real words: e.g., the word *samal* (sergeant) originated as an acronym for *segen mi-chutz la-minyan* ("supernumerary deputy").

5. Israeli natives (literally "cactus pears"). See next section, "Tact versus '*Dugriness*.'"

6. For a more exhaustive interpretation of non-vocal Israeli communication, see the chapter "Gestures" in my book *Israel for Beginners* (Gefen, 2011), 40–41.

in English as a *he* or a *she* according to whether in Hebrew the corresponding word has a male or female humanity.

The natives too, of course, have problems with phonemes that do not exist in Hebrew. The English *th* sound, for example, is obtained by placing the tongue on the upper dental arch and producing a sound linguistically most similar to *dh*. The Israelis work that out in three different ways: some pronounce it as if it were an *f*, some simply replace it with a *d*, and some handle it with a kind of sibilant *z*.[7] Also, they rarely round their lips for *w*. Pronouncing *bowling* a little like "bowelling" apparently sounds too visceral to them, and they instead call this leisure activity *bauwleeng*. The correct pronunciation of the combination *ing* is called a "glued" sound, in which the final *g* is not distinctly heard. Similarly, many English words have silent letters, as in the combinations *kn*, *gn*, *pn*, and *ps* when they occur at the beginning of a word. Hebrew-speakers, however, are accustomed to pronouncing everything they see in black and white (including the vowels that aren't there). Nothing is useless. If a *k*, a *g*, a *p*, or any other letter is there – they reason – there must be a motive and go on pronouncing every letter. They do not leave anything out. They can't help it.

Tact versus "*Dugri*ness"

From an early age, you have learned to communicate through several layers of social conventions and a complex code of civilities. The careful choice of the right words was portrayed as comparably important to a musician's choice of the right notes or a painter's choice of the right colors.

Israelis are very informal in their social interactions, which in many other countries would be equated with plain rudeness. Like the cactus pears to which they are often compared, Israeli natives display a spiny exterior that conceals a tender, sweet core. Unfortunately, under their gruff exterior, some natives conceal several more layers of even gruffer interior. Inevitably, before reaching the Israelis' deep inner core, you will be taken aback by their bluntness, impoliteness, bad manners, and lack of consideration. Israelis, on the other hand, view these cultural attributes in a more positive light. For example, they use a different term for the appalling lack of a buffer zone between what they think and what they say: they call it *dugri*, a word borrowed from Arabic, which means "straight" and is metaphorically used in Hebrew to mean honest, sincere, straightforward talk. What you quite reasonably see as

---

7. A chain of Israeli floristry is called Zer4U. *Zer* means "bouquet" in Hebrew. When Zer4U is pronounced in heavily accented Israeli English, the florists vow to be "*zer* for you!"

a serious attitude problem on their part, they see as a serious perception problem on your part. They do not "argue" with you; they simply explain to you at length and top volume why you are wrong. Years later, once you have become a veteran Israeli, you will meet many Israelis who have good manners. That's precisely the time when you should reexamine your own manners.

Eifo Katuv?

(Says who? Or where is it written that it's forbidden?) This is the Pavlovian response pulled out on you when pointing out to somebody that, for example, he should not throw an empty cigarette package on a public flowerbed. It reflects the native's crystalline notion of legality interwoven with the concept of individual freedom. Is there a sanction for that? Is there a sanction for cutting in front of a long line of people? Is there a sanction for talking loudly on a cell phone in a public place? Is there a sanction for making noise where silence reigns, where the ability to perceive the whisper of the waves or the rustling of the leaves adds an aesthetic value to the landscape? No? Then there is no law infringement. This is neither rudeness nor chutzpah.[8] It is just innate judicial consciousness.

"What Is in a Name?": Calling by Name versus Name-Calling

According to Jewish tradition, names are given by way of divine inspiration, and the essence of every creature is thus found in its name. For the gatekeepers of religion, giving a name is a highly meaningful act and carries an important spiritual significance. Consequently, biblical names have been bestowed, generation after generation, on unsuspecting defenseless babies. Abraham, Isaac, Jacob, Moses, Sarah, Rebecca, Rachel, and Leah are not haphazard names; the character traits they represent are special. This kinship of names is supposed to spur the kid to emulate the virtues of his or her namesake. No one in the religious community would ever entertain the idea of naming his or her child just *Guy* or something similarly impersonal and generic.

God has made an assortment of many millions of different animal species. After making the dinosaurs, the elephants, the giraffes, the snakes, the whales,

---

8. Yiddish for audacity, brashness, effrontery, gall, nerve, etc. Yiddish is a dialect spoken in Central and Eastern Europe as a vernacular by Ashkenazic Jews, written in the Hebrew script. It presents elements principally from medieval German dialects and secondarily from Hebrew, Aramaic, and other sources.

the fish, and the birds, like an artist with no personal style but boundless ambition, He kept trying new ideas. Naming all this previously undescribed wildlife was probably the most creative time biblical taxonomists ever had.

Name-calling used to be particularly spot-on. If you wanted to be rude to people, all you had to do was shout and call them names of zoological characters.

In today's Israel, however, this would rarely work for at least two reasons. Firstly, the natives are used to speaking their mind loud and clear (oftentimes just loud), and secondly, the widespread use of animal-inspired names considerably limits your offense range. In fact, the modern Israeli onomasticon includes: Arieh (lion), Eyal (ram), Dov (bear), Ofer or Ofra (fawn), Rachel (ewe), Talia (lamb), Tzvi (deer), Yael (ibex), Ze'ev (wolf), Ayah (hawk), Baz (falcon), Dror (sparrow), Chassidah (stork), Lilit (night owl), Salit (wheatear), Shachaf (seagull), Tor (turtledove), Tzufit (hummingbird), Yonah or Yonit (dove), Zamir (nightingale), Vardit (rosefinch), Chochit (goldfinch), Re'em (oryx), Gur (cub), Kfir (lion cub), Tziporah (bird), Ayala (doe), Eran (wild goat), Ariella (lioness), Ayelet (hind), Sna'it (squirrel), and many others. Some of these animal-inspired names, such as Devorah (bee), Shunit (reef), and Almog (coral), are not even particularly high in the food chain.[9]

Man is the only animal that feels insulted when called an animal. In Israel, however, unless you descend to the lowest rungs of the zoological scale, calling the natives names from the animal kingdom for insulting purposes defies these very purposes.[10]

---

9. For a more exhaustive list of typical nature-related modern Israeli names, see the chapter "Names" in my book *Israel for Beginners* (Gefen, 2011), 56–64.

10. Cranky scientists all over the world frequently name particularly vile organisms after colleagues they dislike. Most of the time, however, this academic consuetude is considered a form of tribute-giving among researchers. I myself was honored with a pretty disgusting ectoparasitic worm from a Red Sea stingray, kindly named after me by three Australian colleagues: L.A. Chisholm, I.D. Whittington, and G.C. Kearn (2001) *Dendromonocotyle colorni* sp. n. (Monogenea: Monocotylidae) from the skin of *Himantura uarnak* (Dasyatididae) from Israel and a new host record for *D. octodiscus* from the Bahamas. *Folia Parasitologica* (Praha) 48(1):15–20.

Bonding with Loyal Fans

Those who can do.
Those who can't
criticize those who do.
However hard to take,
criticism is often necessary.
It fulfills the same function
as pain does in the human
body, drawing attention to a
possibly unhealthy situation. If heeded
in time, danger may be averted. If ignored, the situation may worsen. As
with pain, there is a threshold of tolerance, which is still surprisingly high
among Israelis as long as criticism is expressed by fellow citizens. That very
same threshold, however, drops abruptly to zero when disapproval comes
from non-Israelis. It may even drop below zero when the non-Israelis are
Jewish. If you belong in this category, you will helplessly watch the locals
freely complain about everything and anything going on in the State of
Israel. *Kvetching*,[11] however, is a pastime that Israeli nationals reserve only
to themselves and should actually be taken as a major sign of normalization.
Spending more time grumbling and less time counting the blessings the
country has to offer means that seventy years have been sufficient for Israelis
to take for granted the great miracle that is their sovereign Jewish state. In
any case, complainers tend to wear themselves out within a short time unless
you are foolish enough to add fuel to the fire by suggesting a hypothetical
solution. Regional problems are so complex that sometimes even native
barbers and taxi drivers do not have all the solutions. As for criticism from
foreigners, the Israelis are known to endure it only as long as it is positive,
unqualified praise.

However deep your emotional connection to Israel may be, even if
you are a fervent Zionist and a frequent-flyer visitor who comes to Israel

---

11. Yiddish expression of whining.

several times a year, even if you feel you are "one of us" but you are not (i.e., you are not an Israeli citizen), you should stay out of Israeli politics. Like fans at a soccer game, Jews around the world have the right and indeed the moral obligation to support the Israeli team. They are expected to do so through every game, every season, every coach, and every player, whether the team is winning or losing. Their emotions need not be wholly rational, just unwavering. Fans may approve or disapprove of game strategies, like or dislike the performance of players in the field, agree or disagree with the coach's choice of players benched. However, only the players play the game.

Hasbarah
(Public Relations)

How Many Light Bulbs Does It Take to Change People?

Hasbarah literally means "explanation." It generally refers to the efforts by the Foreign Ministry's public relations department to disseminate positive information abroad about Israel in the face of anti-Israel propaganda, negative press, and attempts at questioning Israel's right to exist. Alongside public diplomacy, private diplomacy is encouraged. In today's increasingly globalized and interconnected world, every citizen, through his actions and behavior, knowingly or unknowingly can play an important role in shaping the way his or her country is being seen and perceived abroad. Every Israeli citizen traveling overseas is thus called to be an unofficial ambassador of Israel. So innocuous and powerless when they stand in a dictionary, in the hands of a person who knows how to put them together, words can win people's hearts and minds.

Generally speaking, the Israelis have nothing against the most severe critics of their country. Of course, if they only had something that worked, they would use it right away. Anti-Israelism is often anti-Semitism wearing a mask. Fighting against this malignant intellectual cancer should, in truth, be the duty of non-Jews.

If You Can't Convince Them, Confuse Them

Hasbarah is often aimed at countering *taqiyya* (Arabic for concealing, precaution, guarding), an ancient principle enshrined in Islamic doctrine and a Muslim practice to confound and outwit an opponent. According to *taqiyya*, Muslims may freely lie and deceive for the sake of Allah in order to promote Islam.

Understandably, *hasbarah* has been most effective when directed at sympathizers who already share Israel's viewpoints. The impact on all the others, on the other hand, has been relatively modest. This is probably because the approach of the Israeli government is based on the assumptions that ignorance is vincible despite many people's fierce struggle to preserve it, and if the world understood Israel's reality, it would also understand Israel's actions. Unfortunately, the people targeted are often one of a kind (as for what kind, it's easy to imagine) and the truism of the adage "what you don't know can't hurt you" makes them practically invulnerable. As a matter of fact, the Israeli government's approach is based on the erroneous notion that if you broadcast your reasons in high-definition color, even a defective black-and-white TV set will get adequate color reception.

Love and Marriage

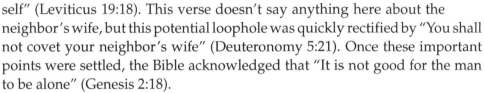

Tying the Knot with an Israeli

The commandment to love other people is given in the Bible, which states, "Love your neighbor as yourself" (Leviticus 19:18). This verse doesn't say anything here about the neighbor's wife, but this potential loophole was quickly rectified by "You shall not covet your neighbor's wife" (Deuteronomy 5:21). Once these important points were settled, the Bible acknowledged that "It is not good for the man to be alone" (Genesis 2:18).

Israel is a country of immigrants, where spouses can be of two kinds: domestic or imported. Transnational marriages have always been permissible in Jewish tradition. Not only there are several instances in the Bible, but accounts of divine punishment of those who did not look favorably upon such unions are reported. Moses' sister, Miriam, who disapproved of Moses' nuptials with Tziporah, a Cushite woman, was stricken with leprosy for criticizing him (Numbers 12:1–10). Not a trivial retribution, considering that antibiotics were still over three millennia away.

Once struck by mischievous Eros, sooner or later, everybody falls in love (falls, mind you – you do not step in love, you fall…).[12] Uncharacteristically defenseless before a chubby winged toddler aiming a weapon at them, Israelis

---

12. In primal times, humans had double bodies – males and females. After discovering that they intended to scale the heights of Olympus, seeking to humble humans, Zeus, the leader of the gods, split humans in half, thus forcing each man and woman to long for each other and wander in search of his/her better half. Eros thus restores what Zeus split. Once the two finally find each other, they feel unified and know no greater joy than that (Aristophanes' speech from Plato's *Symposium*).

are no exception. Love has always been a lovely cruel trick that Nature plays on us for ensuring the propagation of the species.

In modern Israel, cross-attraction between Jewish visitors (the exotic species) and the *sabras* (the native species) occurs frequently. Despite sharing some common heritage, genetic variation between two members of Jewish populations that remained separate for centuries enhances the robustness and quite often the unusual handsomeness of the offspring. Israel is a multicultural society, where people of different backgrounds and languages mix freely.

Marrying an "alien" always provides some extraordinary and enriching opportunities. In families where a parent comes from a different country, the children usually grow up bilingual and are often entitled to dual citizenship. At the same time, this "mixed marriage" deprives the *sabra* spouse of the opportunity to add to his or her stealthy network of Israeli connections and support. When introduced to a foreign spouse's friend, a plain *shalom* and a smile are generally exchanged: no kindergartens, schools, neighborhoods, army units, wars, summer camps, acquaintances, relatives, and so on can be vetted for circumstances in which life paths may have already crossed.

And if you are the exotic spouse, once you settle in Israel, it will be more difficult for you to participate in those traditional class reunions that take place several decades after your teenage years in your country of origin. They are usually organized by a middle-aged former classmate of yours, eager to compare his or her own appearance and professional and personal success with those of all other peers. If you nevertheless manage to go to one of these gatherings, you will discover that most of the people your age seem to be so much older than you. In fact, they will have all gotten so fat and wrinkly that they will recognize you only thanks to your nametag.

When your spouse is a native Israeli and you are not, or vice versa, even if you are both Jewish, the match may present some unique challenges. The disparity of upbringing means that you and your partner view certain aspects of life differently. In addition to the initial curiosity and fascination for the exotic, so many things are new and unusual, interesting and exciting. This is the time you both smile in the same language and sing from the same sheet of music. However, as soon as you start living together as a couple, facing the day-to-day practicalities of life, your different cultures and backgrounds kick in and occasionally clash. You may discover that you are loving a person in a tongue he/she cannot always comprehend – which, incidentally, has nothing to do with the language you are using to communicate with your spouse.

Marriage, Divorce, and Remarriage

Love is supposed to be blind. With time, though, marriage works wonders in restoring sight. And so it happens that some couples realize they actually each married someone else's soulmate. Like socks only theoretically destined to stay paired, they each soon go their separate ways. And yet, poor vision relapses occur, as the majority of people who have divorced go on to marry again. This fully justifies the common practice of Israelis to decline a wedding invitation with a "maybe next time."

Marrying a divorced person is ecologically responsible, as it always pays to recycle. Oddly, some couples who years before were (apparently mis)pronounced man and wife and then split get remarried to each other. Evidently, their divorces didn't work out to the complete satisfaction of both parties. Sometimes, couples do not fully realize what they mean to each other until they have divorced. Some other times, they simply don't want to go through the breaking in of a new mother-in-law. Sadly, their reconsideration is frowned upon in Judaism, as the Bible says "...her first husband, who divorced her, is not allowed to marry her again after she has been defiled. That would be detestable in the eyes of the Lord," (Deuteronomy 24:4). Consequently, such reunifications are not warmly blessed, to say the least, by the Rabbanut,[13] which tends to see them at the same ungodly level as eating shrimp or insects that are not locusts.[14]

---

13. The Chief Rabbinate of Israel has exclusive (and most intrusive) jurisdiction over many aspects of Jewish life, including personal status issues. Secular Israelis encounter religion only a few times in their lives: when they are born, married, divorced, and buried. The rest of the time, they would gladly be exempt from it.
14. According to halakhah (Jewish law), shrimp is a forbidden food, whereas eating locusts is permitted (see chapter "The Bible"). Bon appétit.

Housing

After the establishment of the State of Israel, a large influx of Jewish refugees from all over the world began immigrating to the newly independent state. Many were housed in absorption camps known as *ma'abarot*, meant to provide temporary accommodation. Over time, the *ma'abarot* metamorphosed into development towns. The architecture was determined by the need to give shelter to masses of new immigrants, by the functionality needed to suit Israel's harsh climate, and by the scarcity of natural building materials. Only in Jerusalem, according to an ordinance that dates back to the British Mandate, municipal laws required that all buildings be faced with local Jerusalem stone.[15]

Since those tough times, soaring glass-sided skyscrapers have become part of the landscape in Israel's major cities. Meanwhile, government efforts to introduce affordable housing have never ceased. Nor have housing prices ever ceased to soar. The housing market in Israel is complicated and influenced by a large variety of factors. If the older generations tend to live in the past, it is probably because housing then was so much cheaper. Their dream was to pay off a mortgage on a house in the suburbs. If you are a young couple, your dream today would be to actually get a mortgage, even though by the time you pay it off, the suburbs will no longer be suburbs. Young Israeli families are abandoning the dream of living in a ground-floor house with a yard, as their dream house costs at least twice as much as they dreamed it would. So at the present time, only two kinds of houses are available on the Israeli market: the kind you don't like and the kind you can't afford. Even when you settle for a standard, rather small one-story apartment in the suburbs, this is generally sold to you by the real estate agent as a two-story apartment – one story before the sale, another after it.

---

15. Pale dolomitic limestone, common in the Jerusalem area.

A reasonable amount of money can generally be saved if you buy an apartment in a building that is still under construction. Realistically, however, one thing is the contractor's promises and another is his premises. In other words, you will be lucky if your home will be ready when you are. Apartments under construction are prone to inordinate delays, which the contractor will be quick to blame on the workers. It is a persistent Middle East regional problem nowadays like it was in biblical times. According to the Book of Exodus, the pyramids in nearby Egypt were built by enslaved Israelites under the Pharaoh. As the pointed shape of the pyramids clearly indicates, as time passed, the Israelites tended to work less and less.

Employment

JOB CENTER

Not Quite from the Book of Job

God created the world in six days (which never could have happened if the Histadrut[16] had been there at the time) and then, pleased with His creation, He thought work was a good idea for humankind too. Humankind is still debating whether work is a blessing or a burden. As a blessing, it would make sense to always save some of it for tomorrow. As a burden, it would justify those who don't like to work, but thank heaven, have got jobs, particularly when it takes them the whole week to do a couple of days' work.

Don't Complain if You Have a Job to Complain About

If you are a new immigrant, finding a good job – that is, a job in which your dreams are only moderately clashing with your paycheck – requires first of all overcoming the Israeli companies' tendency to hire natives or at least individuals relatively fluent in Hebrew. Then, you have to bypass Israeli "networking," a well-oiled national grapevine that favors insiders and makes publishing job openings often unnecessary. Finally, being turned down or hired depends on whether you turned up your nose or your sleeves.

In any case, before declining a job offer or quitting a new job too hastily, you should take a good look at both sides: your potential employer's side

---

16. Israel's organization of trade unions and one of the most powerful institutions in the country, which influences much of the wage policy and labor conditions.

and the outside. Israel is a small country and not an inexpensive one to live in. Nowadays, a motivated and talented workforce locally available makes the national job market highly competitive. If you learn to live within your income, you will get along without worry – although, admittedly, without a lot of other things too. But while the disparity between the cost of living and your initial monthly salary may be substantial, getting your "foot in the door" gives you the opportunity to perfect your Hebrew, become better acquainted with your new environment, and whether or not you keep kosher, bring home the bacon.

Hard work never killed anybody, but if you are afraid of being the first victim, then the chances of beating the harsh competition of the natives become slim indeed. Generally speaking, Israelis are an ambitious people, and ambition often gets many of them into a lot of hard work. Driven by a culture of risk-taking in which quick thinking, creativity, and vision are highly valued, Israelis do not consider schedules and deadlines all that important, do not strictly adhere to hierarchy in the workplace, and have no qualms about bending rules to achieve results. Blatant chutzpah is oftentimes exercised, though rarely acknowledged. If you let common sense guide you and suggest doing things by the book, your coworkers may soon start considering you a real *nudnik* (pain in the butt).[17] If your natural attitude toward work has been "if someone else can do it, let him do it; if no one else can do it, how can I do it?" you'll find yourself on a collision course with the natives' "if someone else can do it, I can do it better; if no one else can do it, I must do it" attitude. Problem-solving group discussions among natives may initially appear to you more like loud thunderstorms than creative brainstorms. Even as a new employee, you are expected to demonstrate that you have an opinion by expressing it and defending it. The natives will all acknowledge that you have a sacred right to air your ridiculous viewpoint.

Israelis like to tinker in particular with technology. The end consequence is that a country of eight and a half million people, barely seventy years old, with limited natural resources, surrounded by enemies, in a constant state of war since its establishment, has produced more innovative start-up

---

17. *Nudnik* is a Yiddish word that has entered modern Hebrew. It comes from the Russian *nud-nyi*, which means to bore. In Yiddish, the verb is *nuden*. Fittingly, the Hebrew *nad* refers to rocking movement, and its derivative *nidnud* means a repetitive swinging motion, which graphically describes the annoying persistence of the *nudnik*.

enterprises than larger, peaceful, and more stable nations. Ingenious ideas often degenerate into hard work (which is the disguise opportunities always come in) and perseverance (which is the hard work you keep doing after the hard work you have already done). Of course, in life everyone also needs a bit of luck (which – the harder you work – the more you seem to have).

A Career in Art

A career in the fine arts in Israel is just as black as it is painted. Israel offers a wide range of old and new art-related experiences. Until the beginning of the twentieth century, virtually no tradition of fine arts existed in the country. Early art was mainly decorative and of a religious nature, produced for Jewish or Christian pilgrims. Artists worked with gold or silver and embroidery in small craft workshops.

Today, the visual arts scene in Israel is flourishing, and Israel has become an exciting hub of contemporary art. If you are a modern art lover, you will be impressed by the talent of the many native artists. Israeli modernism in art has explored topics as complex as Jewish tradition versus figurative art and has tackled conflictual questions such as Jewish identity and sociopolitical dialectics. And yet, it is not at all hard to understand Israeli modern art: if it hangs on a wall and does not move or have commercials, it's a painting; if it looks like a 3D printer error and you can walk around it, it's a sculpture. Should you wish to make a living by selling your artwork in Israel, you should consider bank robbery as a complementary pastime to pay your bills.

A Career in Music

Israelis love and enjoy music. Many of them are themselves amateur musicians who play by ear, often forgetting that people listen the same way. Believing that all they have to do is touch the right key at the right time and their instruments will play by themselves, many young natives actually attempt a career in music. Being *sabras*, they have the advantage of being fine-tuned to the musical taste of the younger Israeli generations. Unfortunately, from the melodic viewpoint, the performers themselves are often the ones in need of tuning. Some electric guitar players in particular would be better off plucking chickens than guitar strings.

The economic crisis that followed the collapse of the Soviet Union in the early 1990s and the fear of an anti-Semitic backlash in those turbulent times pushed hundreds of thousands of Russian Jews to immigrate to Israel. Among them was a large contingent of professional musicians. An old joke from an earlier wave of immigration resurfaced at the time: as three Russians come down the steps from the plane onto the tarmac at Ben-Gurion International Airport, one carries a violin case, another a cello case. The one who carries nothing is a pianist.

The government devoted considerable resources to helping these new immigrants to assimilate into Israeli society. A few hundred of the most talented musicians were placed in orchestras by the Absorption Ministry and the Ministry of Arts and Culture. All the others had to suffer an occupational downgrade, for a country as small as Israel could not support them.

In a nutshell, if you play a musical instrument professionally and you are thinking about making a career as a musician in Israel, you should be aware that this market is currently highly saturated. If you are passionate enough about not starving to death, you should face the music, as at the present time your musical talent in this world would most likely qualify you for prematurely playing a harp in the next.

A Career as a Freelancer

As in any other country, many Israelis work better in a set regimen of daily tasks and functions, whereas others are born with an entrepreneurial spirit. *Entrepreneur* is a loanword from French, and entrepreneurship typically begins as a small business conceived by individuals with vision and initiative. As the very large number of Israeli start-up enterprises demonstrates, many entrepreneurs are able to design, launch, and run a business, converting a new idea or invention into a successful innovation. Unfortunately, launching a start-up involves high risks, and a not-negligible percentage of such small businesses fail due to lack of funding, wrong business decisions, insufficient market demand, and so on.

As always in Israel, the more people you know, the better off you are. Being an immigrant in a new ecosystem, not being thoroughly fluent in Hebrew, and not having gone to school in Israel or served in the IDF with all the connections and bonds that those experiences create are serious obstacles to your entrepreneurial journey. They may not be insurmountable, but you must be very determined to succeed. Until then, the natives will empathize with you on being self-employed, which they see as a euphemistic way of saying that you are unemployed.

Israeli Dress Codes

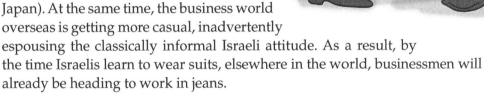

Dressed to the Nines

Although their country has become an international center of fashion and design, Israelis are not generally renowned for their formal attire. Many Israeli companies have been trying for years to push their employees to dress more formally, adopting business dress codes that tradition demands of their international counterparts (e.g., from the United States or Japan). At the same time, the business world overseas is getting more casual, inadvertently espousing the classically informal Israeli attitude. As a result, by the time Israelis learn to wear suits, elsewhere in the world, businessmen will already be heading to work in jeans.

Lawyers

When you feel your rights are violated, exercising forgiveness is usually cheaper but not nearly as gratifying as filing a healthy lawsuit. So if you live in Israel long enough, the day will come in which you will need the services of the only person able to find loopholes even in the Ten Commandments: the Israeli lawyer. In court, Israeli judges wear black robes generally open over a white shirt, black necktie, black trousers, and a black jacket in the winter. Female judges wear skirts instead of trousers, but otherwise a very similar outfit. While generally forgoing the robe, at least in lower courts, lawyers wear a similar outfit. The practice of judges and lawyers wearing such court dress is a legacy of the British Mandate that preceded Israeli independence. The hot weather, the providential fact that wearing itchy scratchy horsehair wigs is not a Jewish tradition, and some residual horse sense have teamed up to prevent this centuries-old British tradition from taking hold in Israeli courts. Outside the courtroom, it will be your suit that will keep your lawyer well dressed.

Police Officers

A police officer in uniform triggers reassurance in law-abiding citizens. The fact that he also carries a big handgun generally triggers a more considerate attitude in the less law-abiding ones. The police uniform inherited by the British Mandate's police force when the state was established included a khaki shirt, shorts stretching down almost to the knees, and socks stretching up almost to the knees. Realizing that a law enforcement officer dressed like a boy scout was less likely to deter Israeli law-breakers, this outfit was replaced by a light blue shirt and dark blue trousers. New uniforms, entirely black and made of rather coarse, wrinkle-proof polyester, have been recently introduced, making Israeli officers look like the tough patrol cops seen in American TV series. Clad in their impressive, dark uniforms in the sunny Middle Eastern climate, inevitably, they have to put up with the annoying question of "Aren't you hot?" which before had always been reserved only for the *charedim*.[18]

Firefighters

A firefighter in full gear triggers reassurance in citizens in need of being rescued. Once simply called *mechabeh esh* (literally fire extinguishers), today, the firemen have adopted the American style and prefer to be called *lochamei esh* (firefighters). Wearing large helmets, goggles, heavy-duty gloves, boots with puncture-resistant soles, overalls with reflective stripes, breathing apparatus, and other impressive paraphernalia indispensable for their noble mission, firefighters have historically given nightmares to young children who happened to be in an already scary situation, such as a burning building. Presentations have therefore been organized in many primary schools in collaboration with the local fire department to familiarize children with the

---

18. The "fearful" [of God] (Isaiah 66:5): ultra-Orthodox Jews living in compliance with a strict interpretation of Jewish religious doctrine. Their standard year-round mode of dress is stuck in early-seventeenth-century Polish rabbinical fashion. Men wear a black suit and a black hat with a black skullcap under it. Women wear long skirts, long-sleeved shirts up to their collarbones, and hair coverings if they're married.

firefighters' gear and procedures and ensure they will be calm and coopera-tive during emergencies and possible Martian invasions.

Paramedics

A Magen David Adom (MDA) paramedic generates reassurance in situa-tions of medical emergency. As a signatory to the Geneva Convention, Israel is an officially recognized member of the International Red Cross. MDA is Israel's emergency medical response organization, ambulance service, and blood bank. Driving on the roads the way they drive, Israelis often make blood available to MDA. Just not their own. Though it currently staffs several hundred medical technicians, paramedics, and physicians, MDA still relies heavily on volunteers. They all wear a white uniform with red-and-silver-trimmed sleeves, red Star of David badges, and on each shoulder, a rank insignia epaulet. All volunteers take a sixty-hour training course that covers a wide range of emergency topics to prepare them for their roles. Those who pass the course join local stand-by first responders in ambulances to provide initial medical treatment and rapid evacuation of people injured (e.g., in road accidents or other disasters). Those who do not complete or pass the course are directed toward administrative duties or other assignments of lesser responsibility. This, of course, is in order to avoid that the first treatment a person already injured receives be administered by someone well meaning but unskilled. In other words, this is done to prevent the term "disaster vol-unteer" from acquiring a strictly literal meaning.

ZAKA Operatives

ZAKA operatives are never a pleasant sight, because their presence is dic-tated by tragic circumstances. An acronym for *Zihui Korbanot Ason* (literally disaster victim identification), ZAKA is an organization of volunteers and emergency response teams. They assist ambulance crews, aid in the identi-fication of the victims of terrorism, road accidents, and other disasters, and gather body parts for proper burial. Most of its members are Orthodox Jews who wear the yellow vests of modern-day rescuers over the traditional black and white clothing that all eastern European Jews wore a few centuries ago. Although the ultra-Orthodox generally segregate themselves from modern Israeli society and are often quite unpopular as a result, the professional man-ner in which these deeply religious men handle difficult and tragic scenes has earned them public respect and admiration.

National Symbols

One People, One Flag, One Snack

National symbols create visual, iconic representations of a people united as a nation. Israel has a national flag (two horizontal blue stripes symbolizing a *tallit* [prayer shawl] with a blue Star of David in the middle on a white background); a national emblem (a shield with a *menorah*[19] in its center, two olive branches on the sides, and the label "Israel" at the bottom); a national anthem ("Ha-tikvah" [the hope], the melody of which has its roots in a popular sixteenth-century Italian song);[20] and national colors (the same blue and white of biblical origin of the flag and traditional colors of the Israeli sports teams playing abroad).

A certain number of unofficial national symbols also exist alongside the above official ones. Numerous other countries elevated an arboreal or floral species to a distinctive statewide emblem (at a time when apples, blueberries, and blackberries were just fruit). Yet other countries have chosen an animal emblem from the local wildlife. Similarly, the State of Israel has elected national representatives of autochthonous flora and fauna. Actually, until around the 1970s, along with shorts and sandals, Israel even had a hat as an

---

19. The seven-branched gold candelabrum looted from the Second Temple in Jerusalem by the Romans in 70 CE. It is depicted in a bas-relief on the first-century Arch of Titus located on the Via Sacra in Rome, just southeast of the Roman Forum.
20. "La Mantovana," aka "Ballo di Mantova" (Mantua Dance) or "Aria di Mantova." The melody gained wide popularity in Renaissance Europe and was used by various playwrights. Most famously, the Czech composer Bedřich Smetana used the tune in *Vltava* (the Moldau), one of the six symphonic poems that make up his "Má Vlast" (My Homeland). Samuel Cohen, a Moldavian immigrant, adapted a Romanian version as the melody for "Ha-tikvah." The poem was subsequently adopted as an anthem by the Zionist Movement at the First Zionist Congress in 1897 and eventually recognized by the State of Israel as its national anthem.

unofficial national symbol: the *kova tembel*.[21] Closely associated with kibbutz[22] life, four triangular cloth panels joined to form a floppy, dome-shaped cap have shielded several generations of Israeli heads from the sun.

An Olive Pitted against an Acorn

In 2007, in a poll conducted among visitors of the popular Israeli news website Ynet, the olive tree (*Olea europaea*) was elected as Israel's national tree. Noteworthy for being one of the biblical seven species of the Land of Israel (Deuteronomy 8:8),[23] it was chosen by the public as a symbol of (however elusive) peace. It outranked the prickly pear (*Opuntia* cactus), known in Hebrew as *tzabar* or *sabra*, the tenacious, thorny desert plant with a tough, thick skin that conceals a sweet, softer interior – the unofficial symbol of the Israeli native. The common oak (*Quercus calliprinos*) finished second, possibly because praises were never sung in the Bible of a little acorn that once held its ground.

Say It with Flowers

Cyclamen persicum is an herbaceous perennial plant that grows wild from the rocky hillsides of Mount Hermon in the north and as far south as the Hebron Mountains. In 2007, it was chosen as Israel's national flower. The plant has heart-shaped leaves and flowers turned downward to protect their pollen from the rain. Because of its beauty, the cyclamen nearly got picked into extinction. Some say this was the reason why, in the language of flowers, the Persian cyclamen must have said something very rude or inappropriate to its many greedy, uncaring pickers. In 2013, a poll was arranged by the Society for the Protection of Nature in Israel and the Ynet website, and the cyclamen was quietly replaced with the poppy anemone (*Anemone coronaria*) as the national flower of the State of Israel. Like its predecessor, *A. coronaria* is an herbaceous perennial plant that grows wild all over Israel. Called in Hebrew *kalanit* from the word *kalah*, "bride," this flower earned its name because it evokes the beauty and splendor of a bride on her wedding day. Most Israelis, however, claim that no one flower can ever symbolize

---

21. Lit. "fool's hat."
22. Lit. "gathering or clustering": a collective egalitarian Israeli rural community.
23. The others being wheat, barley, grape (wine), fig, pomegranate, and date (honey).

their nation and that Israel should be represented by no less than the bride's entire bouquet.

Fowl Election

In 2008, following a national survey, the white-spectacled, yellow-vented bulbul (*Pycnonotus xanthopygos*) was outpolled by the hoopoe (*Upupa epops*), and the latter was declared the national bird of the State of Israel. The elusive dove of peace has always been oddly associated in Israel with a flighty mockingbird and was never a serious candidate for the position. Nor were any of the 530 recorded species of seasonal birds that, by the millions, pass through Israel's skies every spring and autumn. Geese, ducks, cranes, and other migratory birds can often be seen flying in V formation, each bird slightly above the bird ahead, synchronizing their flapping so as to catch the preceding bird's updraft and reduce wind resistance. Ignoring the laws governing drag and turbulence in aerodynamics, Israelis regard this teamwork as a form of organized collective laziness.

As Swift as a Deer

The tan, white, and black mountain gazelle (*Gazella gazella*) is a member of the antelope family, believed to be unique to Israel and a few surrounding countries. It inhabits mountains, foothills, and coastal plains, its range coinciding closely with that of the acacia trees that grow in those areas. The gazelle's beauty, grace, and in particular, its alertness to its surroundings, enemies, and predators make this animal an appropriate symbol of the whole country. Because of its speed and agility, the gazelle was chosen as the logo of Israel's postal service, suggestive of the idea that the postal service would deliver the mail as swiftly as the gazelle. The sloth, which would have been a more accurate logo, was not considered because it is not part of Israel's indigenous fauna.

Every Dog Has Its Day

Little known is the fact that Israel also has a national dog breed. Known in Hebrew as *kelev kna'ani*, the Canaan Dog is believed to have been a feral dog in ancient Canaan and other regions of the Middle East for thousands of years.

The Israelites used it to herd and guard their flocks and encampments, and it is still used by some Bedouins and Druze for this purpose today. The Canaan Dog is a member of the pariah-type dogs, a sub-family of the spitz group of dogs. Its relatively uniform phenotypical traits (size, coat color, structure, and behavior) were recognized as worthy of the designation of dog breed by the Israeli Association of Dog Handlers. In 1966, this top dog was recognized as Israel's national dog breed by the authoritative Fédération Cynologique Internationale.

We Are What We Eat

Being what we eat leaves devout vegans who believe in reincarnation coping with an intriguing reembodiment issue. On the other hand, most Israelis are notorious *mangal* (barbecue) lovers. They enjoy in particular that moment when the seasoned meat sizzles on the grill and a mouthwatering aroma pervades the air. Vegans probably feel the same when they mow the grass.

While we all share that awesome moment late at night when we open the refrigerator and the first thing we see is the snack we wanted to eat (if we're not supposed to eat at night, why is there a light bulb in the refrigerator?), when it comes to food, we all have extremely different tastes.

As a nation of immigrants, in food, Israelis find psychological comfort and a way to stay connected to their pasts. Israel is a special haven for ethnic foodies. Restaurants around the country offer traditional Diaspora dishes in their own time capsules of nostalgia. They start off by opening as local enterprises that cater to a homesick population of recent arrivals. Like oases in the desert, they fulfill a comparable salvation function.

Over time, however, demographics shift and lifestyles change. That is why it is so difficult to resolve the question of what should be considered Israel's national food today. The Israeli gastronomy incorporates many foods traditionally eaten in Levantine, Middle Eastern, and Mediterranean regions, such as falafel (deep-fried balls of ground chickpeas served in pocket-like pita bread), hummus (creamy dip or spread made from chickpeas), and shakshuka (eggs poached in a sauce of tomatoes, peppers, and onions). Despite them all being very tasty, popular with the locals, and a mandatory experience for visitors, honestly, none of these dishes seem inspiring enough to enhance Israel's national identity at home or abroad.

It was suggested that *me'orav Yerushalmi* (a generously seasoned mix of grilled chicken hearts, spleens, and liver), often translated in menus as "involved of Jerusalem,"[24] may also be made more appealing by finding a more creative, extravagant presentation for it. The idea was apparently inspired by the same logic by which a circular pizza cut in triangular slices is still brought to you in a square box. Alternatively, giving these foods more pretentious names may increase their chances of making it to the finals. "Israeli ratatouille," for example, would perhaps make shakshuka sound a bit more appetizing. Admittedly though – as many Israelis coming back from tours in the US have remarked – even buffalo wings still taste to them like chicken.

Meanwhile, in commemoration of the sixty-eighth anniversary of the founding of the State of Israel and the ninety-fifth anniversary of the founding of the Volcani Agricultural Research Center, a poll was held to find out what fruits and vegetables were considered "national" by the country's citizens. The majority of the ballots went to the tomato, considered the "most Israeli vegetable," replacing the orange, hitherto the most popular fruit in Israel. Having never been entitled to grow on a tree like any other respectable fruit, the strawberry was discriminated against in this contest. Although presumably most of the voting members have the wisdom not to put a tomato in a fruit salad, not all of the electorate probably knows that, botanically speaking, a tomato is actually a fruit (the edible berry-type fruit of the plant). One can't help but wonder what tomatoes ever did to make the other fruits disown them and force them to live as vegetables.

---

24. In Hebrew, *me'orav* translates as both "mixed" and "involved."

The Postal Service

The Israel Post is a government-owned corporation that handles postal services in the country. Formerly known as the Israel Postal Authority, its roots are in the postal system from the era of the British Mandate (1920–1948). In April 1948, on the verge of relinquishing their mandate over Palestine, the British discontinued all postal services. The Jewish institutions quickly took over, organizing themselves to print stamps for the state that was soon to be established, but its name (Judea? Israel? Land of Israel?) had not yet been finalized. It was eventually decided that the stamps would read *doar ivri* (Hebrew post). On May 14, 1948, the State of Israel declared its independence. Less than forty-eight hours later, despite numerous problems (lack of printing paper, presses, and perforating machines), the first stamps were issued and sold at postal branches throughout the country.

During these seven decades of Israeli postal service existence, highly developed forms of sluggishness (efficiency) have alternated with less developed forms of sluggishness (inefficiency). The latter have unfortunately increased in recent years. The Israel Post argues that if you were seventy years old, you wouldn't move all that briskly either. Bills actually still travel through the mail pretty fast – in fact, at twice the speed of checks. It has been estimated that today's rate of 2.30 shekels to send a letter within the country includes fifteen *agorot* (Israeli cents) for transportation, fifteen *agorot* for delivery, and two shekels for storage fees. Many Israelis have been complaining about letters delivered late or lost. Unfortunately, their letters of complaint to the Israel Post to draw attention to this annoying problem are delivered late or are lost.

Post offices have been standardized. At the entrance, you must get a number from a touch-screen electronic machine that spits out a slip of paper to you, assigning your position in line. The number of the customer being served at the moment is displayed on a large LCD screen. After comparing your number with that on display, you can make a rough and generally wrong estimate of the waiting time ahead of you. In addition to receiving postal services proper, at the post office, you can pay your car license renewal, utility bills, and even parking tickets. However practical, this bank-like service tends not to enhance your patience when a long wait is foreseen just to pay a bill.

At this point, you either lay bets on some other hopefully less crowded hours and leave, or you resign yourself to a forced long idleness and proceed to join a bunch of other unhappy-looking customers sitting on uncomfortable iron benches. While watching the numbers slowly progressing on the LCD screen, you have to endure the show, played on repeat, of all the new allegedly efficient and timesaving services offered to you by the Israel Post. Meanwhile, you sit and grow older waiting for your turn. Based on the principle that the game Bingo helps elderly people keep their brains alert, the robotic voice of a loudspeaker activated by tired clerks calls out the numbers. The "winner" is then directed to the available teller. The frequent no-shows are an indication that numerous customers have in the meantime either fallen sound asleep or run out of patience and left. Frustration often prevents them from donating their numbered ticket to the holder of a higher number, as local tradition commands.

The Media

Say What You Please

Contrary to other Middle Eastern countries – where one can speak his mind and say anything he wants (at least once) – Israel enjoys a lively, pluralistic, mediatic environment in which free speech and freedom of the press are generally guaranteed and respected. The Israel Broadcasting Authority (in Hebrew *Reshut Ha-shidur*, formerly known as *Kol Yisrael*, the Voice of Israel) was until recently Israel's state broadcasting network, operating eight radio stations and two television channels. This impressive network was shut down, and in 2017, reorganization took place. The new broadcasting body still operates based on the presumption that Israelis are keen viewers and good listeners. The latter is hardly the case, despite the fact that their ears never get them in trouble.

The Radio

The radio is still very fashionable in Israel and enjoys a considerably large audience. Live talk radio in which one can butt in by telephone and interfere with someone else's freedom of speech is a particularly popular format. The right to argue about issues one does not understand is jealously guarded. Unfortunately, in these radio programs, supply of free speech often exceeds demand, and nonsense is quite often delivered to you in at least two languages: Hebrew and profanity. Freedom not to listen, however, is considered just as precious as freedom of expression. Aware as they are that nobody really listens, Israelis feel free to say what they think without thinking, a trait that can be scientifically explained by the law of gravity, as more energy is required to shut one's mouth than to open it. What these freelance opinionists lack in depth, they make up for in length. Technology will one day allow one to run a mouse over them, making a timer-band notification pop up and let any listener know how much longer they're going to babble. At present, only radio sets come with what these wireless human tormentors regrettably don't – on/off switches. The fact that the word *listen* is actually the word *silent* rearranged makes one wonder whether this circumstance is really entirely coincidental. Mizrachi[25] music often fills in the breaks. Some pop songs of this genre never die. But this is not the fault of the radio.

The TV

Veteran Israelis can remember when the roofs of the houses all over Israel were full of antennas and the only bad thing on TV was the reception. The TV sets had a knob marked *brightness*, which some people believed was there to turn up the intelligence of the participants in early television talk shows. It never worked. Today, Israelis who are considering early retirement are advised to watch daytime broadcasts, which always offer first-grade entertainment – in the sense, of course, that these programs entertain those who have not gone beyond first grade. Many inmates who watch TV from Israeli prisons are convinced that the televised programs are part of the punishment. Also, the idea of eliminating violence from TV, debated for some time, was eventually discarded, as that would have meant scrapping the eight o'clock news.

The Press

Although most Israeli newspapers are now also published online, many Israelis are not yet used to reading the newspaper from the screen of a tablet or a smartphone and prefer to browse through an old-fashioned paper journal. Thus, Israel still has a high readership rate of daily print newspapers. Besides, you cannot effectively swat flies with your smartphone.

The Israeli newspapers with the largest circulation are published in Hebrew. *Israel Hayom* (Israel Today) has the largest daily circulation in the country, not only because of the political stance presently more or less shared by the largest sector of the public, but also due to the fact that it is free of charge. *Yedioth Ahronoth* (Latest News) was for many years the largest newspaper in Israel by sales and circulation, followed by *Maariv* (Evening, literally "bringing on night"), followed by the left-leaning *Haaretz* (The Land). This last one is Israel's oldest daily newspaper, founded in 1918 and now published in both Hebrew and English. The *Jerusalem Post* (prior to 1950, the *Palestine Post*) publishes English and French editions.

---

25. Israeli Mizrachi music combines elements from North Africa and the Arab world and is mainly performed by Israelis of Mizrachi descent.

Other newspapers cater to Arabic-speakers, although many such readers are fluent in Hebrew and read *Yedioth Ahronoth* just as easily. Several newspapers in Russian cater to this large group of immigrants (over one million of whom made *aliyah* in the late 1980s when the government of Mikhail Gorbachev opened the borders of the Soviet Union). The new Israeli-born generation has completely assimilated into Israeli society, and although bilingual, prefers to read the Hebrew press. The Cyrillic script, more familiar to the older generations, has a strong appeal to senior readers. Israel's more reliable freedom of the press engenders a refreshing motivation to buy the newspaper.

Israelis from every walk of life often read more than one newspaper. The newspapers enable them to satisfy their keen interest in politics and current affairs so that they can worry about things in other parts of the world. Even religious people, who read the Bible to know what people ought to do, read the newspaper to know what people actually do. A great advantage of Israelis reading newspapers is that the lively discussion and scornful comments they mentally entertain with the author of every article is generally kept on mute or at least "mumble mode," and you don't have to ask them to turn the volume down.

Living with the Threat of Terrorism

When the merciful Good Lord decides for us that one particular day is no longer the first day of the rest of our life but rather the last one, that fateful day will probably begin like any other day. It will just be shorter. When our human physiology is no longer compatible with life, we die. Death is inescapable. Death is hereditary. We should live with it.

We all like to imagine that snag occurring in mature old age, as a result of natural senescence. Sometimes, however, the Good Lord's Angel of Death comes disguised as a brainwashed moron with a *keffiyeh* around his neck who shouts *"Allahu akbar"* before blowing himself up. In the name of a primitive dogma, this bloody terrorist takes upon himself to decide that his last day should also be our last day. He then proceeds to his Paradise to claim his reward of seventy-two virgins, leaving us on Earth to deal with death, mourning, and destruction. Being dead himself now, this apprentice *shaheed* (Arabic for martyr) doesn't know that he is dead, just as he himself did not know he was a fanatical cretin when he was still alive.

As other Western countries are experiencing these days, living with the specter of sudden violent injury or death changes the national psyche. Security in Israel has always been at the forefront of daily life. Counterterrorism methods, checkpoints, armed patrols, bag searches, demographic profiling, and other unpopular or controversial measures put in place by Israel have helped to reduce – but of course cannot eliminate – the threat of terrorism. Consciously or otherwise, Israelis grow up internalizing the thought that there are people out there who mean harm to them, are determined to harm them, and spare no effort to harm them. Israelis are thus typically more circumspect and everywhere more aware of their surroundings than other nationals. And they go on with their lives. This is quite frustrating for Israel's enemies, while it is sometimes commended as a sort of bravery by outsiders sympathetic to Israel. In reality, you'll never know how brave you are until being brave is the only choice you have.

Elections

In highly politicized Israel, voting is an event celebrated with an official national holiday, even though the actual operation will not usually take more than twenty minutes of your precious time. The legal voting age for Israeli citizens is eighteen, an age at which people know everything and can offer those who are older than them the full benefits of their passionate political inexperience. Though the Knesset[26] (Israel's unicameral parliament) is elected for a four-year term, governments seldom serve a full term, and early elections are a frequent occurrence. In high-tech Israel, neither interactive touch screen nor online voting is available. Voting is done using slips of paper as ballots, which is still an improvement over a somewhat earlier procedure that used pebbles or inscribed potsherds.

On election day, you go to your local voting station, which is generally a school in your neighborhood. There, various gangs of supporters wearing different T-shirts noisily remind you for which party you should vote. Avoiding eye contact with any of them, you head straight for the entrance gate. Once inside, by reading makeshift signs, asking around, and bouncing from one classroom to another like a ball in a pinball game, you eventually find the classroom to which you were assigned. You walk up to a table with three people, their attention absorbed in a seemingly endless list printed on continuous form paper. One takes your identity card, another mispronounces your name, and the third one scrolls the list, trying to find your alphanumeric coordinates. Once your identity is established, you are given an official envelope and directed to the voting booth, which is generally a flimsy foldable corrugated plastic or cardboard screen on top of a rickety old table.

---

26. The term Knesset is derived from the ancient Great Assembly (*Anshei Ha-knesset Ha-gedolah*), which according to Jewish tradition was an assembly of 120 scribes, sages, and prophets.

A gentle inadvertent bump with your elbow as you flip a coin to finalize your choice could easily bring this structure tumbling down. Behind it, the secrecy of your political preference is nevertheless secure. From a tray of paper slips with printed Hebrew letters, you select the acronym that represents the party closest to your political views. After putting the ballot slip in the envelope, you walk back to the triumvirate, and before their eyes, you insert the envelope in the secured voting box. Only then you are given your identity card back and you may leave.

During every election campaign, the Promised Land becomes the Land of Promise. It won't take long after the new government takes office before you realize that your earlier perplexities were largely justified, and you should have voted for the party that promised the least so as to be the least disappointed. Your inability to become aroused over the promises of the candidates is a well-known condition, widespread among Israeli constituents. Unfortunately, no "blue pill" has ever been developed for this electile dysfunction.

The Bible

"Because I Said So, That's Why!"

If the Bible were a clear, unambiguous, precise manual for human behavior, as one might expect from the literary effort of a perfect God, a great number of rabbis would have to go to work for a living. Instead, the Bible is a collection of arcane texts written at different times in different locations by different authors who did not bother to proofread their work. Religious Jews consider the Bible to be a product of divine inspiration and an authoritative record of the relationship between God, determined to be involved in what happens in His world, and the human species. They submit themselves to God's commandments, which according to tradition were revealed to the Israelites at Mount Sinai long ago, when they could still safely tour that region.

Also known as the Decalogue, the Ten Commandments are a set of precepts that God inscribed on two stone tablets and gave to Moses. Perched atop Mount Sinai, waiting for God to deliver His directives for ethical conduct and apparently not expecting the engraving of ten short lines to take such a long time, Moses went without food and water for forty days and forty nights (Exodus 34:28). The commandments in the Bible provide the basis for halakhah, Jewish religious law as interpreted by rabbis who have themselves subjugated their minds to the halakhah interpreted by their predecessors, all eager to serve God, although tendentially as advisers.[27] Consequently, the

---

27. The word is derived from the Hebrew root *hei, lamed, khaf* (clear your throat to make the *kh* sound), meaning going or walking, so in a more literal translation, it means "the path to walk on."

original ten, all pithy and to-the-point, eventually ballooned to today's elaborate 613 *mitzvot* (obligations, religious duties). While interpretation of God's word varies considerably between the various Jewish denominations, there is a general agreement among all Orthodox rabbis that God's word is infallible, eternal, and unchanging.

In a country as modern and progressive as Israel, however, where faith in scientific knowledge obtained through reason generally prevails over religious faith, it is perhaps about time to put a question mark where God put a period. An updated and possibly edited version of the Bible, still trapped in a remote primeval time warp, might help straighten out more than a few legalistic aspects of traditional Judaism that have remained unsettled throughout the centuries.

Kashrut

For example, Leviticus (11:6-8) clearly states that eating (or even touching) pork makes you unclean. This dietary violation presumably extends to the entire Suidae family of the order Artiodactyla that includes feral pigs, hogs, and wild boars. All the members of this extended family would have enthusiastically displayed their endorsement of this biblical injunction by giving two approving thumbs up if only they did not have hooves. Despite having halakhically admissible divided hooves, suids have a single-chambered stomach rather than the more complex four-compartment ruminant stomach found in most other artiodactyl families, and thus do not chew their cud. Why the simple stomach structure of this family would make its members untouchable outcasts is not entirely clear, but God's decisions and in particular His ground staff's interpretations are often inscrutable.

Because of their nature, also dragons (Job 30:29), griffons (Psalms 50:11), lamias (Isaiah 34:14), mermaids (Isaiah 13:21), and unicorns (Numbers 23:22, 24:8; Job 39:9-10; Psalms 22:21, 29:6, 92:10; Deuteronomy 33:17; Isaiah 34:7) would not be kosher.[28] This must have been a genuine relief for many a *shokhet* (ritual slaughterer), as slaughtering a flame-spewing dragon might have presented some objective problems. Not to mention the mermaids, which some more liberal rabbis might have also considered at least half kosher.

---

28. Literally fit, proper, clean. Meeting the requirements of Jewish dietary law.

Leviticus (11:10–12) clearly states that eating shellfish is an abomination. Eating insects is also an abomination (Leviticus 11:20 and 23), but an odd exception is made for some members of the order Orthoptera (locusts, crickets, and grasshoppers). In times of famine caused by swarms of these crop destroyers, our ancestors, hungry and in a vindictive mood, evidently overcame disgust and included these insects in the list of perfectly kosher foods (Leviticus 11:21–22). The problem, though, is that more than twenty-seven thousand species of these insects are known today, and only four types – red, yellow, spotted gray, and white – are kosher. Since the rabbinical classifications rely on size and color rather than molecular markers and DNA sequences, it is pretty hard to identify which Orthopterans are halakhically approved to eat.

Crimes Punishable by Death

Certain desecrations are seen without a shred of indulgence in the Bible, and the punishments recommended for certain violations seem to be quite harsh by today's declining and permissive spiritual standards. The major halakhic problem is that both crimes and punishments actually clash with present-day secular Israeli laws. The penalties in particular would be considered exceedingly punitive by the international community, always ready to find Israel at fault for the slightest flaw.

For example, in the second of the five books of the Bible, it is clearly stated that he who works on the Sabbath should be put to death (Exodus 35:2). The third of the five books of the Bible is particularly severe with regard to unlawful sexual relations. In it, it is clearly stated that male homosexuality is an abomination (Leviticus 18:22) and that a gay couple should be put to death (Leviticus 20:13). It is also clearly stated that a man cannot marry both a woman and her mother, and if he does, both he and the two women should be burned with fire (Leviticus 20:14). The indication that relations between a son-in-law and his mother-in-law seem to have been more cordial in antiquity than they generally are in the present day cannot be used as an extenuating factor. Also, a man cannot have intercourse with an animal; if he does, he should be put to death and the animal should be killed (Leviticus 20:15). The latter would presumably be guilty of being a consenting partner enjoying unprotected sex with the human species, so as to avoid the risk of an undesirable pregnancy. Leviticus is no more lenient toward those who engage in excessively unbridled freedom of expression such as swearing, as the whole village can get together and stone the blasphemer to death (Leviticus 24:10–16).[29]

Owning People

On the other hand, the Bible views the principles of property law as benevolently applicable to humans. Classified as property, slaves can freely be bought, owned, and sold. In fact, you can even sell your own daughter into slavery (Exodus 21:7), at least if the price is fair. Joseph was sold by his brothers to the Ishmaelites for twenty shekels of silver (Genesis 37:12–36). It was the same price as a female slave, a reasonable rate considering he was a fit young man. And you can own slaves, both male and female, provided they are purchased from neighboring nations (Leviticus 25:44). Of course, in today's world of economic globalization and online shopping, this market limitation is particularly annoying. Bureaucracy in the Land of Israel has also notoriously grown more and more intricate since biblical times. Unsympathetic toward human traffickers, present-day Israeli authorities would make the application process and related paperwork a real nightmare. Also, due to the tense relations with Israel's neighboring nations, refunds for unsatisfied customers would be practically impossible. One might thus get stuck with a lazy slave who cannot be auctioned off or resold within Israel even at a bargain price. If a slave's will to work needs to be rekindled, however, a modest degree of domestic violence is legitimate: he or she (in full respect of gender equality) can be clubbed to near death if then allowed a couple of days to recover (Exodus 21:20–21).

Rape in the Bible is one of the violations of property law. The victim, of course, is not the woman who has been raped, but her father. The judicial remedy entails a compensatory payment to him of fifty shekels of silver. After this transfer of property, the woman is legally married to the rapist (Deuteronomy 22:28–29).

---

29. Altogether, the Bible advocates the death penalty for thirty-six offenses, including murder, rape, and idolatry. Although the death penalty is a legal option under Israeli law (and was last applied in 1962, when Nazi extermination mastermind Adolf Eichmann was hanged after being convicted of participation in Holocaust-related war crimes), present-day Israeli judiciary does not resort to capital punishment. Criminals who are found guilty of the most heinous crimes generally receive a life sentence for every person killed or maimed. Extra prison terms are often imposed for lesser offenses perpetrated in the course of the crime. These can amount to several years in addition to the life sentence. Of course, the murderers then serve only what they can...

Beards

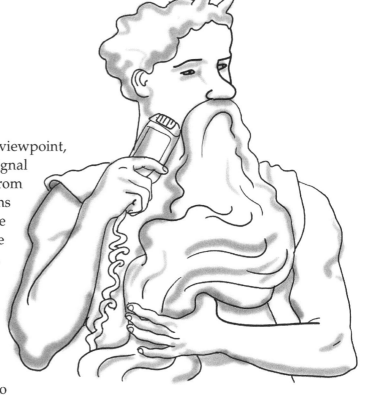

From an evolutionary viewpoint, the beard is a gender signal and a vestigial feature from a time when humans had hair on their face and entire body like our simian ancestors. Since God created man in His own image (Genesis 1:27), the most logical sacerdotal assumption is then that God must also sport a beard. In order to be in good standing with God, any observant adult male Jew must thus be bearded, so as to reflect God's image. Leviticus 19:27 and 21:1-5 give instructions concerning the acceptable fashion of a beard by the Levitical priests and by the general population of Israelite males: the latter are prohibited from "marring the corners of the beard," and the former are prohibited from "shaving off the corners of the beard."

The problem is that a beard naturally rounds to the contour of a face and does not seem to have actual corners. Consequently, since time immemorial, hordes of authoritative rabbis – who obviously had nothing better to do – have been trying to interpret the specifics of this law. Accordingly, shaving the beard with a razor was decreed as strictly forbidden. However, an electric shaver works like scissors, cutting by trapping hair between the blades and a metal grater, and is thus halakhically permissible. Sporting a meticulously groomed beard may not always be enough to enhance male attractiveness, nor would clean-shaven faces help beautify significantly their pallid hues. In order to avoid any unintentional contravening of the law due to an erroneous rabbinic interpretation, the beards of deeply religious men are often left neither tended nor – if you don't consider the food particles that occasionally get trapped in them – nurtured.

Food for Thought

Lost in profound thoughts, sensitive rabbinical souls have, for centuries, delved into the very essence of things. Generation after generation, distinguished rabbis have debated crucial issues. The prohibition of leaving food under the bed (Gemara, *Pesachim* 112; *Shulchan Aruch*, Yoreh De'ah 116) is apparently one of them. As Rashi[30] finally explained, this ban is because of the *ruach ra'ah* (evil spirit) that dwells on foodstuff. However, he ruled that the problem only applies to cooked foods and people who sleep throughout the night, whereas leniency is to be applied in cases of quick snacks or short naps.

Why the zombies of Haitian folklore, always most eager to feast on human brains, would walk right past the architects of such enlightening sanitary warnings stands explained.

---

30. Acronym for Rabbi Shlomo Itzchaki, an authoritative medieval French rabbi, author of comprehensive commentaries on the Bible and on the Talmud.

Science

Intellect over Zealotry

The great development of science in the last decades has been accompanied by an alarming increase in the number of things we know nothing about. Scientists live on the boundary between what is known and what is unknown; their mission is to push this boundary deeper into the territory of the latter, painstakingly but steadily effacing what is not yet understood.

Tiny Israel is a giant in scientific research and has a reputation for high-quality science. Ten Nobel Prizes have been awarded to Israelis – not a negligible achievement for a country of just eight and a half million people. Four have been in the field of chemistry. Three of the Nobel laureates in chemistry were graduates of the Technion, which is located in the northern port city of Haifa and often cited as Israel's equivalent of the prestigious Massachusetts Institute of Technology (MIT). Israel's fourth chemistry laureate came from the Weizmann Institute of Science in Rehovot (near Tel Aviv), one of the country's leading research institutes. Other Weizmann researchers have won the prestigious Wolf Prize in medicine, a common predictor of the Nobel Prize. One of the advantages of being an Israeli scientist, apparently, is that you don't let common logic get in the way of doing things everyone else knows are impossible.

Any prestigious prize awarded to a countryman of theirs generates in the Israelis a profound sense of national pride. Their psyche is quick to turn an obvious individual achievement into the perception of a collective accomplishment. Congratulations are thus graciously accepted countrywide.

Israel has one of the highest ratios of university degrees to population in the world. Twenty-four percent of citizens in Israel's workforce hold university degrees, and 12 percent hold advanced degrees. Israeli academics also publish more scientific papers per capita than anywhere else in the world. Israel may not yet have internationally recognized geographic borders, but at least in science, its national boundaries do not exist at all. Israeli scientists collaborate with colleagues abroad, competences are pooled, and new knowledge is produced and shared to enhance human enlightenment and progress.

Ignorance Can Be Cured

Stupidity is forever. It knows no barriers of time or place. There is no rehab for it. Some people are born stupid; others broaden this natural attribute of theirs over the years, step by step. Some particularly receptive individuals let stupidity be thrust upon them. Whether spread horizontally (from one individual to another within the same generation) or vertically (from parent to offspring), when intellectual defenses are low, stupidity can be highly contagious.

Unfortunately, it is never lethal. Carriers are rarely asymptomatic. In fact, they are often emotional, noisy, and most annoying. They are also strategically distributed so as to fulfill God's plan for you to encounter them at a rate of at least one a day.

When stupidity is associated with ignorance, the syndrome is particularly devastating. Affected people often react by turning their lives around: from ignorant and stupid, they evolve into becoming stupid and ignorant. Regrettably, not nearly enough biomedical research has been devoted to finding a remedy for this tragic cognitive condition.

Bacteria, fungi, protozoans, and other forms of primitive life are very common on Earth, whereas intelligent life is fairly rare. Actually, certain regions of the Middle East seem to be totally incompatible with this latter type of life. In the areas where a waste of two billion years of evolution is painfully evident, science has still a long way to go to free simple minds from bigotry, superstition, and obscurantism, whose lethal combination can often be seen in action.

The well-known *March of Progress*[31] drawing of fourteen apelike forebears of man in a parade depicting the road to modern *Homo sapiens* fails to present the many present-day humans who didn't quite make it to the fifteenth figure drawing. Never letting education get in the way of their ignorance and compulsive rituals, these human evolution dropouts live with their feet in the twenty-first century and their heads in the Middle Ages. While making use of their heads just to grow hair and dandruff, only a tad beneath their

---

31. Famous scientific illustration of twenty-five million years of human evolution. It was commissioned by Time-Life Books for the Early Man volume (1965), authored by anthropologist F. Clark Howell and the Time-Life editors.

scalps, abstruse fantasies, prophets, messiahs, angels, and demons rage. Justifying the unjustifiable by believing in events that do not square with reality, in facts that contradict the laws of nature, and in a powerful god always on their side, these people are an inspiration to morons worldwide and living proof that human IQ can attain negative peaks.

The more zealous they are, the more cocksure they are that they know precisely how everyone's lives should be modeled to their own religious codes. Angry at those who are indifferent to the will of their god, they act like they believe God would act if He only knew all the facts. Brandishing a holy book in one hand and a dagger in the other, they endeavor to drag everyone else with them into the Dark Ages. When the theory was formulated that nothing exists in nature without a purpose, those individuals were obviously not taken into account.

Greek, Roman, Norse, and many other mythologies are encouraging evidence that religions are not everlasting and that enlightened human minds are eventually able to separate fact from fiction. Scientists have always been most sympathetic with Adam and Eve and have long forgiven our unfortunate ancestors for having eaten the fruit from the Tree of Knowledge (Genesis 2–3).

Technology

"If I have seen further, it is by standing on the shoulders of giants."[32] Sometimes great ideas need the foresight of other ingenious people to develop. The wheel is a classic example. The human who invented the first wheel was undoubtedly crafty, but the one who invented the other three was the real genius.

The goal of technology is ostensibly to create a more comfortable future for humankind. The greatest developments of technology in the last decades have apparently been made by lazy people looking for easier ways to do things. When these inventors were also clever and ingenious, the results were utterly amazing. The most humiliating consequence is that we are now surrounded by gadgets that are smarter than we are.

Israel has one of the world's most technologically literate populations, endowed with problem-solving ingenuity and creative talent. Often regarded as applied science, technology is one of the country's most developed sectors.[33] It's so advanced, in fact, that some Israelis brag that when they look back, they see the future. Israeli scientists and engineers have generously

---

32. Attributed to the twelfth-century French philosopher and scholar Bernard of Chartres, this metaphor was notoriously Isaac Newton's favorite expression. The image of dwarfs standing on the shoulders of giants humbly expresses the fact that new discoveries and inventions are often made by building on previous ingenious ones.

33. Israel ranks second in the world in innovation according to the World Economic Forum's competitiveness report. Proof of how well deserved this high rank is is demonstrated by IDE Technologies, a world leader in water desalination founded in 1965 by the Israeli government originally to address drought issues. Probably foreseeing that in a few decades global warming might make it easier to sell ice to the Eskimos, this Israeli company produces innovative snow cannons that can shoot eight hundred cubic meters per day of high-quality snowflakes. One has been in use at the Pitztal ski resort in Austria and another at the Zermatt ski resort in Switzerland.

contributed to the natural sciences, life sciences, agricultural sciences (in particular in arid and semi-arid zones), weaponry, medical devices, information technology, and cyber security, as well as to a multitude of areas in electronics. The field of robotics, for example, has improved to the point that in a few years, one robot is expected to do the work of ten robots. Advancement in computer sciences has also been particularly fast. This advancement is best illustrated by tablets, which in their earliest version did not come with a touchscreen display, were much heavier, and had only Ten Commandments, downloaded from the cloud.

Rainy Days

"I Shall Send You Rain in Its Season…"

In the ancient Land of Israel, rain was literally a vital concern. A good rainy season meant a good harvest and plenty of drinking water, while a severe drought meant famine, thirst, disease, and death of livestock.

In many societies around the world, rain dances, prayers, and other weather modification rituals have been used extensively to increase rainfall. Jews, too, have embraced this early sort of meteorological procedure and have been praying for rain for millennia. To this day, prayers for rain give expression to the natural anxiety felt in the Land about drought, which is regarded in the Bible as a punishment from God (Deuteronomy 11:11–17; I Kings 17:1).

The prayers for rain are recited sixty days after the beginning of halakhic autumn, but not before Shemini Atzeret,[34] because rain should not be invoked when fine weather is needed to enable Jews to dwell in relative comfort in the sukkah (Talmud, *Sukkah* 28b). This schedule is strictly observed by all religious Jews everywhere, because their prayers are meant to fulfill the needs of the Jewish nation as a whole. Which, of course, includes the Jews living in the southern hemisphere, where the seasons are reversed. For a reason that science has not yet been able to explain, Jewish prayers seem to have always been more effective south of the equator, where monsoons, cyclones, typhoons, and other violent weather disturbances almost regularly deliver

---

34. The eighth and last day of Sukkot, the Feast of Tabernacles, instituted by God as a way of reminding Israelites in every generation of their deliverance by Him from Egypt. During Sukkot, observant Jews dwell in booths or tabernacles that are made from the branches of trees as their ancestors did in the desert (Leviticus 23:40–42).

the most intensive deluges on earth. This has led some devoted Jews living in the southern hemisphere of Earth to recommend that the supplicatory fervor of Jews living in the northern hemisphere of Earth be somehow moderated, and that a global ceiling should be set with regard to the magnitude of any precipitation invoked.[35]

Located in a semi-arid region of the northern hemisphere, Israel has suffered from a chronic water shortage for years. There are no large rivers. The average annual rainfall is five hundred millimeters, which is concentrated mostly in four or five months of the fall and winter and mostly in the north-central part of the country. Periods of multi-year droughts or near-droughts have not been infrequent. The relatively steady increase in the population, extensive industrial growth, and fair economic development have placed a continuous and growing pressure on Israel's limited water resources.

Consequently, rainy days in Israel have never been considered inclement weather. Quite the contrary, they come as a blessing to both those who save up for them and those who don't. In a country otherwise divided on many political, religious, and cultural issues, nothing can please and unify the entire population more than the news that the water level of Lake Kinneret[36] has risen a couple of inches. It is a kind of selfless gratification at a national level. Israelis at large may not all fully comprehend the importance of rainfall for the stability of the ecosystem, but they are all happy when on TV they see the Kinneret Limnological Laboratory scientists delighted by the lake's refilling. Local tourist operators are happy when they can confidently count on enough water at the baptismal site frequented by Christian pilgrims. Local fishermen are happy when they can hope for fishing at least half as good as that in Jesus' times, when fish multiplied so easily and Jesus was able to feed the multitude.[37]

---

35. Nothing better expresses this necessity than an old Italian idiom: *"Troppa grazia sant' Antonio!"* (roughly: "Too much blessing, St. Anthony!"). As the legend tells it, the sentence was uttered by a short-legged friar who wanted to ride his donkey but always failed to build up the necessary momentum to climb onto the animal's back. After several desperate attempts, he appealed to his favorite saint, invoking his grace. Then, he tried again, and this time, powered by a sacred furor, completely leaped over the donkey's back, painfully landing on the ground on the other side. Turning again to the saint, he moaned that the grace he had been granted was far too much.
36. Lake Tiberias or the Sea of Galilee, Israel's main freshwater reservoir.
37. According to the Gospels, Jesus was able to feed a crowd of between four thousand and five thousand people, all in a single rally, starting from nothing but two small fish and five loaves of bread: a fact that, two millennia later, undoubtedly inspired the size of restaurant portions when *nouvelle cuisine* met molecular gastronomy.

Of course, the innate predisposition of the Israelis to complain takes over quickly, and as soon as the rain stops, people start grumbling about the mud or the sudden floods. After particularly heavy downpours, some natives even claim to have seen animals beginning to pair up.

Desalination: The Dream of Lot's Wife Come True

Whereas some spiritually inspired people pray for more things than they are ready to work for, others activate their brains, take action, and find solutions. Thanks mainly to a breakthrough in membrane technology that has made desalination much more efficient and cost effective, today, Israel gets 55 percent of its domestic water from desalination. Combined with wastewater treatments that recapture 86 percent of the water that goes down the drain and use it for irrigation, desalination has made Israel water independent, no longer relying on a short rainy season to replenish its limited supplies. In fact, Israel now produces more freshwater than it actually needs. From Moses parting the Red Sea (Exodus 13:17–14:29) and making drinking water spring by tapping a rock with his rod (Exodus 17:6) to Jesus walking on the Sea of Galilee, the ability of Jews to perform miracles with water has become legendary.

Rolling Back the Desert

"The best time to plant a tree was twenty years ago. The second-best time is now," says a Chinese proverb. Sometimes, thousand-year-old proverbs seem like they were penned for today. In the Israeli fast-paced lifestyle in which the present moment appears to be the only thing that matters, this ageless adage is as relevant as ever. Tree planting is actually an ancient Jewish tradition. When you plant a sapling knowing that you will unlikely be able to nap under the shade of the full-grown tree, more than greening and beautifying the land of your forefathers, you are nurturing the land of your offspring.

All over the world, more and more forests are destroyed every year for timber or to make the land available for agriculture or urban use. Deforested areas frequently degrade into wastelands. With more than two hundred forty million planted trees, Israel has been combating the encroaching desertification in the region and preventing soil erosion. Israeli forests are the product of massive afforestation efforts coupled with water conservation and forest management plans by the Jewish National Fund. When the State of Israel was established in 1948, forests covered only 2 percent of its territory. Today, trees cover 8.5 percent, approximately one hundred thousand hectares, which is astounding in a country that is 97 percent drylands. Shade provided by trees planted in the desert has been reducing evaporation of the sparse rainfall.

Even a new hobby is acquiring popularity in Israel, widespread in many central European countries: mushroom picking![38]

Israel's gain of thousands of hectares of woodland per year was accomplished in spite of devastating fires caused by the irresponsibility of some hikers, warfare, and frequent arson by hostile elements and terrorist attacks on this invaluable man-made bio-resource. Whether caused by imprudence or spite, nine out of ten fires were allegedly started by humans. As for the tenth, one has to believe that there must be a malicious hedgehog out there who knows how to strike matches.

---

38. Some four hundred species of mushrooms are known in Israel, of which about forty are edible. Pickers generally focus on just three varieties: Oranit (*Suillus granulatus*), Nartikanit (*Volvopluteus gloiocephalus*, syn. *Volvariella volvacea, Volvariella speciosa* var. *gloiocephala*), and Segolit (*Laccaria amethystina*). The most appreciated Gushit Ne'echelet (*Boletus edulis*) and Gevionit Ne'echelet (*Cantharellus cibarius*) are found only in oak groves, only in the north of Israel, only in the winter, and are extremely rare. The desert truffle Kemahit Afrikanit (*Tirmania africana*) grows in the late winter at a depth of ten to fifteen centimeters under the sand of the Western Negev desert by the roots of *Helianthemum* spp. in symbiosis with these shrubs.

Boycott of Israel's Academia

I can manage without Zionist technology!

The Hatred of Idiots: A Sign That Israel Is on the Right Path

Several proposals have been launched by the Palestinian Campaign for the Academic and Cultural Boycott of Israel (PACBI), calling for an international boycott to be imposed on Israeli academic institutions. The ultimate mission of the academic boycott aligns with that of the greater Boycott, Divestment, Sanctions (BDS) movement, a loosely connected group of activists and organizations coordinated by the Palestinian BDS National Committee, which rose to prominence in the mid-2000s. BDS engages in a vicious campaign of defamation and delegitimization by depicting Israel as a racist, fascist, totalitarian, and apartheid state. The campaign is designed to ostracize Israel internationally so as to increase economic and political pressure on the Israeli government and thus force it to exercise more favorable policies toward the Palestinians. According to its official website, the movement seeks to end the "occupation and colonization of all Arab lands," but in fact, it wages economic warfare only against the Jewish state. Under the auspices of the BDS movement, the activists speak the same language in which in the 1930s people were called upon to not buy from Jews in Nazi Germany. The boycott movement against Jewish businesses was the prelude to the Holocaust.

When Education Begets Bigots

Deeply indebted to their imagination for facts, brainwashed, and biased, the activists of this movement seem to have nothing left in their right brains and nothing right in their left brains. Their efforts to demonize Israel and turn the clock back to the time before the Jewish state was created are obstinate and unrelenting. Cleverly disguised as responsible academics, these fellows are often pro-Palestinian students and – worse – professors of colleges and universities in several European and North American countries in which education is supposed to make cultural standards higher. While far better science and technological know-how are emerging from Israel than from these scholars' academes, these diehard bigots make incitement to boycott Israeli academic institutions the ultimate mission of their miserable lives. However minor the harm to Israel's economy may ultimately be, these despicable individuals nevertheless play their heinous, vitriolic, irresponsible part. No single snowflake ever considers itself responsible for the avalanche.

There are not enough middle fingers to express the contempt BDS engenders in the average Israeli. The movement has nevertheless been tarnishing Israel's image internationally. While downplaying the damage caused by BDS activities, the Israeli government has allocated substantial funds to more forcefully thwart the hostile actions of BDS. While in itself an acknowledgment that BDS has become more than a nuisance, the government countermeasures act on the same principle by which a mosquito bite itches less when you manage to swat the mosquito.

It is at least to be hoped that all the money that the BDS movement saves local academic institutions by preventing scientific collaboration with Israeli researchers is put to good use, possibly to buy all the BDS supporters many, many medicines for their personal use (as Jews, when we tell someone to go to hell, then we worry about him getting there safely).

Israel's "Never Again!"

…Against Israel's Enemies "Never Say Never"

Israel's enemies are distributed around the globe in a rich assortment of politically, ideologically, religiously, and racially motivated foes, whereas incinerating bolts of lightning on the globe are not distributed correctly. Hence the Israel Defense Forces (IDF), the military arm of the State of Israel, comes into play. The name was chosen because it conveyed the idea that the army's role was *haganah* (defense), and because Haganah was the name of the pre-state paramilitary organization upon which the new army at the time was formed. The IDF's raison d'être is not so much protecting the land of our forefathers as preserving the land of our children. Today, the IDF structure consists of ground forces, the air force, and the navy, headed by the chief of general staff, who is subordinate to the defense minister.

The IDF is one of Israeli society's most prominent institutions, heavily influencing the country's economy, culture, and political scene. In addition to Jewish soldiers, it includes Israeli Druze, Christian Arabs, and an increasing number of Muslim Arabs. The IDF adheres to a rigorous moral code of conduct that affirms the preciousness of life in the face of enemies who teach their children a culture of martyrdom. Other differences from all other armed forces in the Middle East include the mandatory conscription of women and their option for deployment in combat roles. Israel's regular army is relatively small, and thus its strength in emergencies is based on reservists, who comprise a large chunk of the entire nation.

Si Vis Pacem Para Bellum

(If you want peace, prepare for war).[39] Israel spends nearly 20 percent of its national budget on defense, which would make this old Latin aphorism more correctly translatable as "in times of peace, prepay for war." A large percentage of the defense budget goes toward technology research. The IDF uses several high-tech weapons systems developed in Israel, many of them made specifically to meet the IDF's needs.[40] The IDF possesses top-of-the-line weapons and computer systems, sophisticated cameras and surveillance systems, and precision-guided munitions. Israel is also the world's largest exporter of unmanned aerial vehicles, more commonly known as drones. The Star of David that Jews were forced to wear in Nazi Germany is now on Israel's fighter jets. Within the foreseeable future, piloted combat aircraft will be phased out of service by drones capable of carrying out nearly any aerial operation. Satellites capable of guiding ammunition are being developed. Weaponry is continuously improved. Old models are replaced by more practical and more effective ones. Since its founding in 1948 following the establishment of the State of Israel, the IDF has been specifically designed to match Israel's unique security situation. The overall concept is that if you deal with a problem before it becomes a problem, you may have already gotten the solution under way, an ideology based on the stark reality that – unlike its enemies who are used to losing wars – Israel cannot afford to lose a single one.

The Israel Defense Forces drafts all Israeli citizens at the age of eighteen. The normal length of compulsory service is currently three years for boys and

---

39. Vegetius, *De Re Militari*; late fourth century CE. A similar concept is expressed by Niccolò Macchiavelli (Florentine Renaissance historian, politician, diplomat, philosopher, humanist, and writer, considered the founder of modern political science) in *Il Principe*: "The ideal condition for a prince is to be at once loved and feared, but if you cannot have both at once, it is preferable to be feared."

40. Such as the Merkava main battle tank, the Akhzarit armored personnel carrier, the Iron Dome missile defense system, the Trophy active protection system for vehicles, the Galil and Tavor assault rifles. The Uzi submachine gun, invented in Israel, was used by the IDF until 2003, ending a service that began in 1954. Reconnaissance robots, similar to a cross between a miniature tank, a miniature bulldozer, and Number Five (from *Short Circuit*, John Badham's 1986 movie), are being introduced to the infantry brigades. These machines are likely the precursors of combat robots. The IDF has close military relations with the United States, including development cooperation, such as on the F-15I jet, the Nautilus or THEL laser defense system, and the Arrow missile defense system. Israel also flies the largest contingent of F-16s outside the United States, with close to three hundred jets. All the aircraft have been heavily modified with Israeli-made avionics, self-protection systems, radar, and advanced weapons.

two years for girls. The IDF determines a medical profile for you, according to which the army decides where to assign you. The highest profile is ninety-seven. If you receive the lowest profile, twenty-one, you are considered unsuitable for military service and are fully exempt from it.

The IDF does a better job at guaranteeing the cultural and physical future of the Jewish collective than religion ever did anywhere in the world. Nevertheless, if you are a *yeshiva* (school of Talmudic studies) student, you can claim that if God had meant for you to be in the IDF, you would have been born with drab, baggy olive skin. With this indisputable argument, you can receive deferments as long as you continue your religious studies. In practice, you will end up never fulfilling this obligation and you will thus become a successful draft-dodging divinity scholar.

"Nation will not take up sword against nation, nor will they train for war anymore"

Until Isaiah's prophecy comes to pass, having a clear aim in life is always important. In Israel, you should also pair a good aim with knowing when to pull the trigger.

If you are drafted, once you complete your mandatory military service, you will serve in a reserve unit in accordance with the army's needs. If you immigrated at an older age, the IDF tends to make your military service less arduous. You will undergo a relatively short period of basic training, after which time you will be assigned to the reserves and called up – in peacetime – for a few weeks a year. During these stints (*miluim*), you will be joined by other fellow soldiers that form your unit, many of whom are Israeli natives. As a new immigrant, you will soon begin wondering whether your comrades are there for business or pleasure (or both). For many older natives, in fact, *miluim* is often a period of actual relaxation, a quite pleasant break from routine. Family responsibilities and daily stress at the workplace are temporarily put on hold. This is the time when – while wearing battledress – insurance agents sell insurance packages, businessmen offer special deals, professionals propose their services at a bargain price to their comrades in arms, and even joint ventures are formed.

Incidentally, this is also the time when you discover that in your tent those who snore always fall asleep first, and that being reprimanded for a dirty magazine has nothing to do with stashing a *Playboy* magazine in your sleeping bag, but rather with having the magazine of your rifle soiled. Also, you will find out that coffee tastes better if the latrines are dug downwind from the encampment.

The Shekel

Wealth, they say, is not the key to happiness. Let alone poverty. At least if you have enough money, you can always have a spare key made. Money cannot always buy you happiness, but then again, happiness can never buy you groceries.

For millennia, cattle (which included sheep, camels, and other livestock) were the only trusted currency.[41] The real step forward in monetary history took place around 2000 BCE in the Middle East. Money was originally a form of receipt, representing grain stored in temple granaries in ancient Mesopotamia and Egypt. It took a while for humans to gain confidence in a currency that did not possess an intrinsic value and was not edible but was easy to preserve and transport.

The Hebrew word *shekel* is actually based on the verbal root for "weighing" and may have originally referred to a weight of about 180 grains (eleven grams) of barley. As early as the year 2085 (counting forward from Creation), Abraham bought Sarah's burial site from its owner Ephron the Hittite for four hundred shekels of silver.[42] The shekel was common among western Semitic peoples. It was used during the United Monarchy of Israel (1050–930 BCE), the Kingdom of Israel (930–720 BCE), and the First Jewish-Roman War (66–73 CE, aka the Great Revolt). In 1980, replacing the Israeli lira, which had been the currency since 1948, the shekel was reestablished as the currency of the modern State of Israel. Since the 1980s, the Israeli economy has strengthened, and even the Israeli citizens have become stronger. At that early time, it took two people to carry fifty shekels worth of groceries. Today, a child can do it.

---

41. In the Roman world, each head of cattle was called a *caput*, Latin for "head." So a person with a lot of cattle had lots of *caput* or "capital," a word still used today to describe money.
42. Genesis 23. The burial site was the Cave of Makhpelah.

One hundredth of a shekel is called an *agorah*. The name, suggested by the Academy of the Hebrew Language, was borrowed from the Bible (I Samuel 2:3), where the word is used in the phrase *"agorat kesef"* to describe a piece of silver. This low-value denomination has never been adopted into Hebrew with the same figurative connotations as pennies have in English. For example, "a penny for your thoughts" is a polite way of asking someone what he's thinking about, often used when a person has been quiet for a while. However, Israelis generally do not stay quiet for long whiles. Similarly, you should not use the expression "where can I spend a penny?" to inquire where the closest urinal may be, because coin-operated public toilets were never introduced in Israel. The expression "my two cents," which stands for "my humble opinion," never stood the chance of being translated into "my two *agorot*," because Israelis rarely view their opinions as humble. Belittling your own opinion is a diplomatic approach intended to preemptively mitigate a possibly confrontational statement. However, diplomacy is a trait rarely displayed in ordinary Israeli discussions. Even when an Israeli says "I may be wrong, but…," he does not really believe that such a possibility actually exists.

The Israeli shekel is available in the form of coins and banknotes, both produced in South Korea, since Israel does not have a mint.[43] Discussions about design, images, portraits of prominent personages, and use of polymers for the new-generation bank notes went on and on, but at least a few good points were raised: a tactile set of dots to help visually impaired and blind people identify denominations. In 2008, the twenty-shekel banknote, printed this time in Switzerland, was the first denomination made of polypropylene that went into circulation in the country. These technological improvements rendered life more difficult for those who used to make a lot of money rather than earning it (the counterfeiters). The polymer substrate also dramatically improved the life span of banknotes in circulation. Unfortunately, it did not lengthen their life span in your wallet in any appreciable way. In the vola-

---

43. Actually, it does, although it only issues commemorative coins and medals. The Israeli Mint has minted special coins for the *pidyon ha-ben* (redemption of the firstborn son). The *Shulchan Arukh* (Code of Jewish Law) states that a father must "redeem" his firstborn child from a *cohen* (Hebrew for "priest," traditionally believed and halakhically required to be of direct patrilineal descent from the biblical Aharon, Moses' brother, representing the original Temple priesthood) for the sum of five silver shekels. Each coin contains 23.4 grams of silver, five of which come to the required 117 grams of silver. In Judaism, this is a *mitzvah* (commandment, religious duty) in which the original animal sacrifice is replaced by a less gruesome monetary offer.

tile Middle East, things tend to get rapidly out of hand, and apparently, that includes your hard-earned money. Money talks, they say. Unfortunately, yours also walks and often says goodbye. When you are a new immigrant, any "street smarts" you may think you brought with you from your native country drop to "Sesame street smarts" level in Israel. With arguing and bargaining capabilities dreadfully underdeveloped, you will be amazed at the natives' ability to estimate the cost of a service performed within a shekel or two of what you have in your pocket.

Banks

"Wine maketh merry, but money answereth all things" (Ecclesiastes 10:19).[44]

Israel has a quite sophisticated banking system. The Bank of Israel is the government's central bank. It issues currency, supervises all Israeli banks, and regulates banking policy. Bank Leumi (formerly Anglo-Palestine Bank, established in 1903), Bank Hapoalim (established in 1920 by the Histadrut, Israel's organization of trade unions), and Bank Discount (formerly Palestine Discount Bank, founded in 1935) are Israel's three largest banks. Along with First International Bank, Bank Mizrahi-Tefahot, Bank Otsar Ha-Hayal, Union Bank of Israel, and a few other minor ones, they are the providers of private banking services in the country. In recent years, banks have not sprouted new branches as they used to. This is due not only to the fact that it was ascertained long ago that money does not grow on trees, but also because most ordinary transactions can today be made online from your computer or mobile phone.

Inevitably though, either because you want more from your bank (in which case the only way would be for you to rob it) or possibly out of concern more for the return *of* your money rather than for the return *on* your money, sometimes you will have to physically go to the bank and interact personally with the manager or a cashier. Banks in Israel are only open five hours a day, Sunday through Thursday mornings, and they offer a few additional ever-crowded afternoon hours a couple of days a week. Once again,

---

44. King James translation.

Israel endeavors to be at the forefront, even when it comes to setting inconvenient banking hours. In fact, the hours when you are generally free and can stop by the bank dovetail perfectly with the banks' closing hours. Also, ATMs may occasionally swallow or disdainfully spit out your card, but unlike human tellers, at least they do not have the unsanitary habit of moistening their thumb and index fingertips on their tongues to count the bills before handing them to you.

Shopping

Time Is Money, so When You Go Shopping Take a Lot of Time

Israel manufactures a wide variety of products. Tourists and newcomers have the opportunity to stroll up and down the aisles of big supermarket chains and check out unique local specialties. Handicrafts usually cost less near where they are made, so you should buy olive-wood handiworks in Nazareth, religious items in Jerusalem, Bedouin handiworks in Beer Sheva, malachite jewelry in Eilat, and T-shirts with Hebrew slogans and other cheap Israeli souvenirs in China.

The *Shuk*

A *shuk* is an open-air marketplace popular with natives and tourists alike. Mostly food (fresh fruits, vegetables, fish, meat, cheeses, nuts, seeds, spices, wines, liquors, etc.) but also clothing, shoes, housewares, textiles, Judaica, and a large variety of other goods are sold in the stalls of a typical Israeli *shuk*. The vendors' shouting about their wares to passers by is all part of the banter and bustling atmosphere. From an evolutionary viewpoint, the *shuk* is the precursor of the modern-day flea market, supermarket, and shopping mall, with the difference that prices tend to be flexible, depending on the vendor's mood, persuasive ability, and above all, the customer's language or foreign accent.

The *Makolet*

A *makolet* is a small grocery store, located in your neighborhood or within a walkable distance from it. It is often a family-run business. Struggling to survive the irrepressible wave of large and inevitably cheaper supermarkets, some are open twenty-four hours a day. There, you can buy bread, milk, eggs, and stuff you suddenly discover you ran out of. Since nobody really buys nonessential groceries at the *makolet*, if you decide to do so, you should check their expiration date because they have probably been on the shelves since the *makolet*'s festive opening day in the mid-1980s.

The Supermarket

The weekly grocery shopping is done by most Israelis at the supermarket, where the cart is temporarily turned into one of the most expensive-to-operate vehicles in the country, and courtesy is generally limited to the automatic doors that open for you.

Most food items come in sealed packages to discourage the natives' natural instinct to tamper with the product by sniffing it or quietly tasting it before proceeding (or not) with the purchase. Israeli food companies had to come to terms with the landfill spaces filling up in a country as small as Israel, so they adjusted the packaging of many products to be more environmentally friendly. For example, milk is packed today in practical recyclable cartons. Still available in some supermarkets, however, is milk packaged in old-fashioned uncontrollable plastic bubbles, similar to blood transfusion bags, that require a pitcher to hold them with a low-front *V*-shaped cleavage to control the spout.

Eggs are sold in unsealed cartons of recycled paper pulp molded in dimples and accommodating twelve eggs. This structure is meant to protect the eggs by absorbing possible shocks exerted during transportation. However, since eggshells are fragile and Humpty Dumpty-style accidents occasionally occur, the natives make sure they are not buying broken eggs by gently tickling every single egg out of its dimple. If the egg sticks to it, it means that at least some egg white has leaked out and glued the shell to the dimple. The egg's refusal to dislodge is an indication that the egg had already cracked up before you tickled it.

Until not long ago, flimsy plastic grocery bags were freely available at the checkout. In a national effort to reduce the devastating impact of polyethylene on the environment, today, by law, you are charged ten *agorot* for every bag. Charging a fee on plastic bags has not improved their quality. They are still of the kind you have to blow on the top or rub vigorously to pull the damn edges apart while the cashier is drumming her fingers waiting for your payment.

The Shopping Center

The word *kanyon* entered the Hebrew "slanguage" and is now used in Israel to describe any covered shopping center. It is a play on the word *koneh*, which means "buy," and *chanyon*, which means "parking lot" and refers to the large parking area around the mall. Since it ends up sounding like the English word *canyon*, several of the malls that in the last decades have sprung up all over the country have been named the Grand Canyon after the Grand Canyon in Arizona, one of the Seven Wonders of the World. (Not surprisingly then, the majestic Niagara waterfall straddling the border between the United States and Canada inspired the name for the standard Israeli flush toilet.) Israelis go to the mall mainly for the entertainment value. In general, they don't have in mind anything in particular they need to buy there, but they rarely come out empty-handed because every department store offers the stuff that Israelis don't need at a price they cannot resist. Several fast food chains opened branches there, serving their greasy, salty, high-cholesterol specialties and sugar-filled sodas to loyal customers who are already showing distinctive signs of mall nutrition.

Cannabis

Medical cannabis appears to be somewhat effective in treating chronic pain and some neurological illnesses, easing the symptoms of post-traumatic stress disorder and reducing chemotherapy-induced nausea. Under the control and supervision of the Ministry of Health, medical use of cannabis has been permitted in Israel since the early 1990s for cancer patients and those affected by illnesses such as Parkinson's, multiple sclerosis, and Crohn's disease. The Israeli government's progressive legislation regulates the entire medical cannabis supply chain, including real estate for cultivation, commercial marketing, extraction of bioactive compounds, delivery devices, clinical trials, treatment, manufacturing, patient management, and potentially, export. Meanwhile, Israeli academia[45] is carrying out more research to find out whether, in the long run, the psychoactive chemical components that help alleviate pain also pose significant health risks, particularly to young people (older people always complain anyway about their joints).

Arguing with the police that you had said "no" to drugs, but the drugs just wouldn't listen is not going to exonerate you if you are caught selling or growing marijuana, which remain criminal offenses. The government, however, is mulling over giving the green light to decriminalizing the use

---

45. The chemistry and pharmacology of cannabinoids have been studied intensively by a research group headed by Prof. Raphael Meshulam of the Hebrew University of Jerusalem. A former Weizmann graduate and a distinguished member of the Israel Academy of Sciences, Prof. Meshulam was the first scientist to identify, more than forty years ago, the main psychoactive constituent in cannabis (tetrahydrocannabinol, THC). He and his team of collaborators, PhD students, and post-docs are credited with the isolation, structure elucidation, and synthesis of several other major phytocannabinoids.

of marijuana. This drug notoriously causes psychic alteration and increases the risk of accidents if a person drives a motor vehicle while intoxicated. The Israel Anti-Drugs and Alcohol National Authority (IADA), the governmental law enforcement agency responsible for fighting the plague of drugs and the destructive consequences of drunkenness, has issued severe warnings to keep off the grass. The potential for abuse associated with the legalization of cannabis is so real that the High Holidays in Israel may soon lose their spiritual connotation. People for whom no clear line exists between religion and use of marijuana, instead of "Hi, how are you?" might soon greet each other with "How high are you?"

In actuality, use of marijuana does not make you stupid. If you smoke it for recreational purposes, it means you were stupid before you smoked it.

Tourists in Brief

Invasive Species

Tourists infest every corner of the globe. Between three and four million of them visit Israel every year. Tourists are of two kinds: vacationers and travelers. The latter set out to meet local people, appreciate the culture and history of the places they are visiting, and expand their vision of the country. They come to realize how vast and how small Israel can be at the same time. All the others are holidaymakers. Despite the globalization of costumes and lifestyles, stereotypical traits still stand today that distinguish the various nationalities.

Arab Tourists

Recent years have seen a dramatic rise in the number of visitors from Islamic and Arab states that have no diplomatic ties with Israel. They arrive both through Ben-Gurion Airport and through the border crossings with Jordan. The majority of them arrive in the country for religious reasons, but some also come for business, shopping, and curiosity. Arab tourists are surprised to find out that Israelis know quite a number of Arabic words (mostly bad ones) and use them in normal Hebrew conversations. After an initial understandable wariness, Arab tourists abandon the sensation of being constantly monitored by the secret bolice (police) and quickly feel cun-fort-a-bull (comfortable) touring the Jewish state.

Italian Tourists

The remarkable thing about Italians abroad is that they are usually noticed. Not always for the best reasons, but always and everywhere they make themselves immediately recognizable. A seafaring people, Italians love to travel. Even if they do not speak the local language, they can be the most rowdy and loud, even when the only way they can reasonably communicate is by gestures. Since these features are also very much Israeli, these two Mediterranean peoples seem to have quite a lot in common. If it weren't for their stylish clothing and vowel-rich melodic language, Italians in Israel would pass completely unnoticed.

Scandinavian Tourists

The leading Scandinavian airline (SAS) discontinued its daily flights to Tel Aviv in 2000 after the Second Intifada kicked off and a period of intensified violence ensued. The rarefaction of blond, fair-skinned, Danish/Swedish/Norwegian dream women has been particularly hard on many Israeli guys.

Well isolated in their polar latitudes, Scandinavian peoples developed weird food tastes. They also developed a disappointing anti-Israel political stance. With regard to politics, they have been totally impervious to Israeli *hasbarah*. At least on the food front, Scandinavian tourists are able to appreciate falafel, shakshuka, and hummus. Given that they consider *lutefisk*[46] a delicacy, that might have not been surprising after all.

British Tourists

After leaving Israel in 1948 at the end of the British Mandate of Palestine, the foggy Albion islanders are coming back as disinterested tourists. They are the most polite and appreciative of all visitors until their first experience with Israeli rudeness, which generally occurs within minutes of landing. They tend to look in the wrong direction for oncoming traffic before crossing the street. They distinguish themselves by getting quickly sunburned. The color of the British tourist will tend to shift from pink to cherry red and finally stabilize on light purple. They long for eggs, sausages, baked beans, and watery

---

46. Marinated cod, notorious for its intensely offensive odor.

coffee at breakfast and strong Earl Grey at teatime. Late in the evening, they become very appreciative of Israeli beers (or any other foreign brand).

German Tourists

They speak a language that consists of twenty-yard-long words, bristling with hard consonants. Some of them are wary of making it heard in a country whose establishment is to a great extent linked to the Holocaust. Sandals with white socks, however, immediately identify tourists as German (a small margin of error may be caused by Russian tourists). Germans tourists look like tourists even to other tourists. In the middle of winter, they dive with nonchalance in the waters of Med Sea, Red Sea, Dead Sea, or Lake Kinneret at temperatures considered polar by the locals. They are ready to eat dinner at five-thirty in the afternoon, a time that, for most Mediterranean peoples, comes just after breakfast.

French Tourists

They move through Israel as if subjecting the country to a critical examination. Anywhere they happen to be, whatever they happen to see is tested against some undefined but very high Gallic standard. They are not particularly surprised to find out that Israelis today eat more crispy baguettes than soft pita bread, and they are unimpressed by the fact that the Israelis produce (or try to reproduce) many kinds of cheeses. The cheese variety in Israel has not yet reached the hundreds, which according to General Charles De Gaulle was evidence of the impossibility of governing his people. In fact, Israelis were difficult to govern even when the available variety of cheeses was limited to white cheese and yellow cheese, and the available variety of political parties was limited to Labor and Likud.

American Tourists

Dressed in outfits reminiscent of Sunday golfers, they can generally be heard before being seen, their presence often heralded by some "Oh mah Gawd!" They are relaxed and confident in most circumstances, as long as those circumstances are coming at them in English. Dumbfounded when they realize that non-English speakers actually do exist, they up the volume, repeat themselves, and speak slowly in a condescending effort to be understood. They order authentic falafel and look for the ketchup dispenser. They are forever expecting ice cubes in their soft drinks and free refills. They always seem surprised to find out that you can actually buy things with shekels, which they regard as Monopoly money. They believe Israelis give a hoot about their ancestry ("My great-great-grandfather was Jewish").

Canadian Tourists

Normally quieter and more soft-spoken and reserved than their southern neighbors, Canadians stick their iconic maple leaf on clothes, backpacks, and suitcases so as not to be mistaken for American Yankees. They are upset by the average Israeli's lack of concern for that important distinction. They claim they can speak some French as long as they don't have to prove it. They pretend to be overwhelmed by the Israeli scenery and landscapes. They are actually underwhelmed but far too polite to point out that all the forests, streams, and mountains the Israelis are proudly showing them wouldn't count as a backyard garden back home.

Australian Tourists

Friendly mates, Australians are wrongly convinced that they speak understandable English. Aussies use words that were common in Ireland and southeast England over two centuries ago that have fallen out of usage ever since and abbreviations that make no sense outside of the land down under. They share with Israelis the same passion for spending a relaxing arvo (afternoon) outdoors grilling meat on a barbie (barbecue). They take their steaks medium, rare, or medium-rare, while Israelis frantically fan their coals to grill massive quantities of meat for large groups of family and friends until the meat is charred, carbonized, or charred-carbonized.

Asian Tourists

Chinese visitors are relatively easy to recognize: they are short, travel in huge parties, and smile constantly. Japanese groups are revealed mainly by the women, as they all wear large sunglasses and carry parasols. They shoot selfies from their cellphones at a rate that brings to mind the firing of a submachine gun. They complain about the hotel beds being too high and too soft. They must be repeatedly reminded that a brusque "no" is the most polite way Israelis say "no."

Ben-Gurion International Airport

It's a small world, but access to it for many Israelis requires getting first to Ben-Gurion International Airport. After founding the State of Israel and serving as its first prime minister, Ben-Gurion is today the largest international airport in the country and is often referred to by its acronym in Hebrew: Nutbug (*Nemal Te'ufah Ben-Gurion*). It is operated by the Israel Airports Authority, a government-owned corporation managing all border crossings.

With the onset of mass immigration from Ethiopia and the former Soviet Union in the 1980s and '90s and the increase of international business and tourism travel, Terminals 1 and 2 became painfully inadequate, prompting the building of Terminal 3, a state-of-the-art terminal inaugurated in 2004 and today Israel's main gateway. Millions of passengers pass through it every year. Foot traffic is organized in a triple-layered system: departures on the upper floor, arrivals on the ground floor, and a railroad track on the underground floor. In this complex, a long corridor is particularly impressive: a huge, shatterproof glass partition separates the stream of incoming visitors from the stream of outgoing travelers, each heading in the opposite direction. Although probably not in the architect's intentions, the narrative of Jacob's ladder comes oddly to mind.[47]

---

47. "He had a dream, and behold, a stairway resting on the earth and its top reaching to heaven, and angels were ascending and descending on it" (Genesis 28:12).

Like any other airport, and even more so due to the small size of the country and its Jewish character, Nutbug is a place of great energy and most contradictory emotions: anticipation, excitement, joyous reunions, and a familiar voice shouting your name, or painful goodbyes, awareness of soon being miles away from your loved ones, and the sudden switch from the familiar to the foreign. Whichever the case, hugs and kisses there are the most heartfelt and sincere you can ever give or receive in your life.

The velvety female voice on the airport's loudspeaker system, on the other hand, never betrays the slightest emotion in its announcements of arrivals and departures, unless of course it is superseded by the frantic call of ground personnel urging travelers to immediately reach their departure gate. These latecomers are normally Israeli passengers flying for the first time. When asked by the check-in counter operator the standard question, "How many travelers are flying with you?" they usually reply, "How would I know?! You should know! It's your damn plane!" They start their vacations overseas even before leaving the ground, enthusiastically shopping at the airport's duty-free store. They also hoard chocolate, cookies, and other snacks for the plane, given that charter airlines have recently begun to charge for everything except for the bad service, which is still free. Affordable all-inclusive low-cost trips cover multiple destinations. If these laggards manage to eventually catch their flights, they will have breakfast in Athens, lunch in Zurich, dinner in Amsterdam, heartburn in London, and baggage in Rome. Psychologically going nowhere, they always and surely reach their destinations. Once returned from one of those once-in-a-lifetime vacations (i.e., never again!), they realize how good it is to be back home where people who criticize their crude behavior at least do so in a language they can understand.

Electric Bicycles

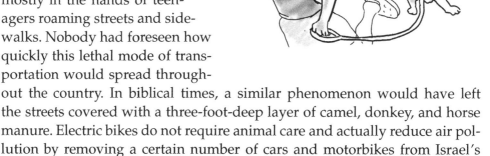

The people of Israel have been recently smitten with a post-biblical eleventh plague of near-Pharaonic proportions: a swarm of thousands of electric bicycles mostly in the hands of teenagers roaming streets and sidewalks. Nobody had foreseen how quickly this lethal mode of transportation would spread throughout the country. In biblical times, a similar phenomenon would have left the streets covered with a three-foot-deep layer of camel, donkey, and horse manure. Electric bikes do not require animal care and actually reduce air pollution by removing a certain number of cars and motorbikes from Israel's roads.

Unfortunately, this modern-day green alternative has also removed a certain number of pedestrians from the sidewalks. Gone are the times when a bicycle had its passenger as its sole engine and could only go three or four times faster than pedestrians. The integrated electric motors used for propulsion in e-bikes can be quite powerful and allow this modern velocipede to hit speeds of thirty to forty kilometers per hour. Most of the riders are unruly Israeli youngsters going through that juvenile stage that in many cases lasts until they reach age fifty. Riding these self-propelled bikes like Baron Munchausen rode a cannonball, these rascals zip by, startle, near miss, graze, hit, hurt, and knock down pedestrians. Electric bikes run smoothly and silently. The pedestrian will hit the ground before knowing what has actually hit him. So technologically advanced are the latest shock absorbers that the rider can hardly feel the bump when running someone over.

Following a series of serious accidents involving electric bicycles, teenagers, and normal people, the Israeli Ministry of Transportation has set new regulations. Minors under sixteen are banned from riding these bikes, and the speed limit is set at twenty-five kilometers per hour. Riders must wear a helmet always and a high-visibility vest after sunset. Police officers have the right to deflate the tires or confiscate the battery of an electric bike ridden by an offender. Making blissfully whizzing kids heed a whole new set of regulations, however, has proven to be difficult, since Israeli kids serenely and routinely disregard both conscientiousness and traffic laws. Police can only enforce the latter.

Road Signs and Markings

Clearly, the importance of road traffic safety is a concept not new to the region, as putting up road signs has been encouraged since biblical times: "Set up road signs; put up guideposts. Take note of the highway, the road that you take" (Jeremiah 31:21). Today, road signs fall under the responsibility of the Ministry of Transportation, and they generally have the same pattern of colors, shapes, and symbols as those used in most European countries. An exception is the stop sign, which conveys its halt command through the depiction of a raised hand. Other typically Israeli signs not to be encountered in Europe are those that warn you of the presence of stray camels along the road or the risk of poor visibility due to sudden dust clouds raised by crossing armored tanks.

Information and destination signs are generally written in Hebrew, Arabic, and English. The Romanization of Hebrew – that is, the use of the Latin alphabet to transliterate Hebrew words – has given way to a large and creative variety of different spellings for the same location or street name. This is a problem that has always driven street mappers nuts and is unlikely to be resolved anytime soon. Probably not before an agreement is reached on how to spell Hanukkah (Khanukka, Channuka…).

Another still unresolved problem is how to interpret time frames underneath parking signs. The many "No Parking" signs in the cities are responsible for keeping an already dynamic country such as Israel constantly on the move. Parking signs are usually accompanied by an explanatory legend. If you can read Hebrew, you may think you know now that parking there has the time frame of, let's say, "6:00–18:00." At this point, though, the question arises of whether you should read it right-to-left like the rest of the sign or left-to-right like in regular math. In other words, whether parking is permitted or forbidden during the span of time indicated by the sign is a fifty-fifty chance.

Finding a parking place in the city centers may be one of those miracles for which the Holy Land was once renowned. However, you had better take a look at the color-coding on the sidewalk curb to make sure you did not rejoice prematurely. There are a few parking rules that you must heed. An unpainted curb means that you found one of those increasingly rare zones, the Holy Grail of parking: free parking. Red and white stripes mean no parking. Red and yellow also means a no-parking zone for you unless you drive a public bus. Blue and white stripes mean parking is subject to a fee or is only available for permit-carrying local residents. Parking fees can be paid at roadside vending machines that will spit out a *kartis chanayah* (parking fee receipt). Most natives in major cities use an electronic "pay to park" system called Easypark or a smartphone app called Pango. It is unclear what black and white curb markings actually mean, but you had better not park there. This is in spite of the fact that the natives generally consider the black and white markings to mean "parking tolerated when no other space is available."

As a visitor or new immigrant, you will be able to keep track of the major Jewish holidays because they are the ones on which alternate-side-of-the-street parking is suspended. You will generally become familiar with parking rules and payment methods only after you get your first parking ticket. And you will quickly become an expert in these procedures if your car is towed away.

Public Health

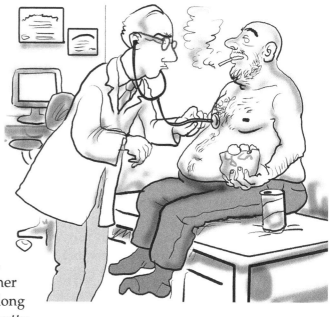

Health makes wealth. The other way around, on the other hand, rarely works. Generally speaking, if you can put up with the inevitable by-products of socialized low-cost medicine – the multitude of forms to fill out, the standing in line with other melancholic patients, the long waits for your turn, etc. – pretty good medical care is available to you. Although biomedical studies haven't yet figured out some way to make your ailments as interesting to your doctor as they are to you, it is reassuring to know that when necessary you can rely on an efficient medical service. Even so, it is a bit scary that doctors still call what they do "practice." Collateral assistance to patients is also quite good; in all the hospitals throughout the country, breakfast is served to you in bed. The earliest sign that you are ready to leave the hospital is when the strictly kosher food begins to taste good. And undoubtedly, there is no better place than home for convalescence – that is, the period when you are still sick after you've gotten well.

Since 1995, health insurance has been mandatory. Medical services are provided to members through regional hospitals and local clinics of four health insurance companies, known as *kupot cholim* (sick funds): Clalit, Maccabi, Meuchedet, and Leumit. This system enables you to have diseases that would otherwise be beyond your means. Without it, only wealthy people could afford to get sick, and less wealthy people could only afford incurable diseases. Although health services always leave room for improvement, Israel's high-quality medical technology, modern hospital facilities, and fairly adequate ratio of physicians to population all contribute to the country's relatively high standard of health today. Which is good, considering that the practice of medicine has advanced so much in recent years that it is now impossible for a doctor not to find something wrong with you.

General health throughout the country would further improve, of course, if the Israelis would simply give up at least some of their bad habits (e.g., smoking, eating grilled grease-dripping meat, leading a sedentary life, etc.). But Israelis are very persuasive people. They can convince themselves of anything. First, they are firmly convinced that their bodies will last them a lifetime, so there is no real reason to worry about old age. Second, they realize that good health simply creates the slowest possible rate at which they can depart this life. And last, many of them do not quite see the point of keeping healthy by eating what they do not want, drinking what they don't like, and doing what they'd rather not do so as to live long enough to become an absolute burden to their loved ones.

The Twilight Years: Retiring

No More Days Off and Coffee Breaks on Your Own Time

According to Israeli law, once you reach the venerable age of sixty-seven, you become the equivalent of a perishable item that has reached the *best if used by* date. Sixty-seven does not look as old to you as it used to. And yet, you are invited to make room for the less knowledgeable, less experienced, less qualified younger generation and join the wobbling force of the *pensionerim* (retirees). At your workplace, your colleagues will organize a farewell party, the size and warmth of which will depend on the relationship you have maintained over the years with what most retirees nostalgically refer to as their "second family." A big cake with your name spelled in cream or chocolate on top will be custom baked and presented to you. Your colleagues will jokingly complain that the candles actually cost them more than the cake. You'll smile, but a disheartening thought will cross your mind that had they placed all the due candles on it, the cake batter could have baked itself.

Until a few years before, you were a busy bee. You'd wake up in the morning with plenty to do, and by bedtime, you'd have it only half-done. Once you retire, you wake up in the morning with nothing to do, and by bedtime, you have it only half-done. You become more aware that age has claimed a toll on your body. Now that you finally have the time to chase your dreams, you're in no shape to be running. Every time you go to the beach in your bathing suit, you can feel everyone around you dressing you with their eyes. The big break you have always dreamed of in life is now likely to involve one of your creaking bones. The bucket list items that you thought "I ought to do before I die" are becoming part of your oughtobiography, an account of your personal life you are unlikely going to write. Your wife, who is now getting twice as much husband on half as much income, begins to realize she never gave your secretary enough sympathy.

As soon as you retire, negotiations start with Bituach Leumi (National Insurance Institute of Israel – roughly the equivalent of Social Security in the United States) and whichever life insurance company manages your pension funds. These are generally the two bodies responsible for the disbursement of your pension after a lifetime of contributions. Your inclusion in their database and establishment of your monthly allowance (that is, the amount of money you will be underpaid) are characterized by official letters with various options to choose from and directives worded in such a way as to make the oracles of Delphi sound, in comparison, like crystal-clear phraseology. The procedure takes into account scores of factors, is quite lengthy, and since presumably it is the first time that you have retired, several terms used are unfamiliar to you. The length of such documents defends them from the risk of being read. Seeking advice from the natives, who at the very least should have an easier understanding of the language of the Ten Commandments, is not generally of great help, as native Israelis are notorious for harboring opposite opinions on the same subject simultaneously. This is the time to start more aggressively planning for your retirement, which includes playing the lottery between three and five times per week.

Retirement: An Exhausting Occupation

The recognition process of your new senior citizen status requires you to run around to government offices, municipality offices, utility offices, banks, and so forth, wading through their morning and afternoon customer reception hours, climbing stairs, waiting in line with other lost souls, being bounced from one office to another, from one clerk to another, from one teller to another. You will be surprised to realize how helpful the obstacle course training that you learned long ago in the military has suddenly become. The art of negotiating obstructions by running, jumping, and climbing in an urban environment was further developed into an actual discipline by the French, who called it *parcours* or *parkour* (pardon my French). Unfortunately, your arthritis prevents you from fully enjoying this sport.

Aging is a fact of life and a privilege denied to many. Each day, they say, is like a gift. Strangely, this gift often appears as if it were made by someone who got your size wholly wrong and didn't bother to include a return receipt.

Bituach Leumi expects you to take comfort in the fact that old age doesn't last all that long, and you have to go through it only once. Whoever manages your pension funds invites you to adopt a more philosophical attitude and change your perspective on what really matters in life, which often consists of the little things, like your pension. If you had dreamed of not working and having a lot of money, you must admit that at least 50 percent of those dreams have come true.

Epilogue

Reading books makes emigrants of us all. It takes us away from where we are, and for an hour or two, brings us to another reality, sometimes to exotic lands we would not have otherwise thought of visiting. This book took you on a short virtual trip to Israel and you briefly encountered its unique people.

Life in Israel is full of unpredictable events, even more so in the life of a new immigrant. If you decide to settle in Israel, let your sense of humor be your sword, your shield, and your armor that will protect you along the bumpy road to integration. The inevitable stressful situations you will encounter are magnified by the unfamiliar environment. Staying in high enough spirits when you can't really see anything laughable about what's happening to you will help you defuse tension and provide you with a more realistic perspective. Let your eventual success be your best revenge. As soon as possible, though, get rid of your armor: you cannot grow in it. Be positive and optimistic. Israel is a young country; the cement is still fresh, and you have the opportunity to leave your personal footprint in it. Whatever you may think, no footstep is so small that it does not leave an imprint.

Acknowledgments

If the book is a hit, I'd like to thank my wife Barbara, without whose unquestioning support and encouragement this book was nevertheless written, and my friends Norman Shachar and Robert Chasan, who went through the trouble of reading the entire manuscript and offered most constructive suggestions.

Unacknowledgments

If the book is a flop, I'd like to dedicate it to nobody and in particular to those reviewers who received a free copy from the publisher and offered useless and nasty comments.

About the Author

Angelo Colorni was born in Mantua, Italy, in 1947. In 1973, he moved to Israel. Fascinated by the Israelis, he has been studying the species in its natural habitat ever since. A marine biologist and senior scientist at the Israel Oceanographic and Limnological Research, National Center for Mariculture in Eilat, he is the author of numerous research works on diseases of aquatic organisms published in prestigious scientific journals. Married to an American wife, he sees himself as an Italian Israeli, his two children as Italo-American Israelis, and his grandchildren as Israeli Israelis.

About the Illustrator

Avi Katz, an award-winning artist, illustrator, cartoonist, and caricaturist, is a graduate from the Bezalel Academy of Arts and Design in Jerusalem. Avi has illustrated many books, and his vignettes regularly grace the pages of the *Jerusalem Report* magazine.

BY THE SAME AUTHOR
Gefen Publishing, 2011, 146 pages

Israel for Beginners

A Field Guide for
Encountering the Israelis in
Their Natural Habitat

Angelo Colorni

GEFEN PUBLISHING HOUSE